PLACE IN RETURN BOX to remove this checkout from your record.
TO AVOID FINES return on or before date due.

DATE DUE	DATE DUE	DATE DUE

MSU Is An Affirmative Action/Equal Opportunity Institution

c:\circ\datedue.pm3-p.1

Tenancy Relations and Agrarian Development

Tenancy Relations and Agrarian Development

A STUDY OF WEST BENGAL

SANKAR KUMAR BHAUMIK

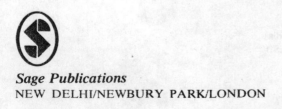

Sage Publications
NEW DELHI/NEWBURY PARK/LONDON

To My Parents

First published in 1993 by

Sage Publications India Pvt Ltd
M-32 Greater Kailash Market I
New Delhi 110 048

Sage Publications Inc
2455 Teller Road
Newbury Park, California 91320

Sage Publications Ltd
6 Bonhill Street
London EC2A 4PU

Published by Tejeshwar Singh for Sage Publications India Pvt Ltd, phototypeset by Pagewell Photosetters, Pondicherry, and printed at Chaman Enterprises, Delhi.

Library of Congress Cataloging-in-Publication Data

Bhaumik, Sankar Kumar, 1956–
    Tenancy relations and agrarian development: a study of West Bengal / Sankar Kumar Bhaumik.
        p.   cm.
    Includes bibliographical references and index.
    1. Land tenure—West Bengal (India)   2. Farm tenancy—West Bengal (India)
I. Title.
HD876.B447   1993   333.3′23′095414—dc20   93–7495

ISBN: 81–7036–344–6 (India)
       0–8039–9118–5 (U.S.)

Contents

List of Tables

Foreword

Economic literature is replete with studies on agrarian problems. No other area of research has touched upon as many issues concerning rural life and people as studies on agrarian economy and relations. Thanks to the numerical preponderance of rural populations in most of the developing countries, such studies have been of immense value for policy formulation and rural reforms over different historical periods. Among the numerous agrarian issues, the problems associated with exploitative tenurial relations have received great attention. In particular, the problems of share-crop tenancy have held centre-stage. As research on agrarian realities started growing in the post-war era, a plethora of grass-roots realities came to public attention, focusing on the specific historical variations in agrarian structures across regions and on the intervening role of public investment in rural infrastructures and technical change. Spatially speaking, the most intensively researched area in India has been West Bengal. This is understandable because Bengal has been a classic case for the suffering caused by exploitative agrarian policies during the British regime; and also by the occurrence of acute natural disasters from time to time. Naturally, the agrarian studies on West Bengal have thrown up a lot of unanswered questions. Thus, a long chain of continuing research issues awaits a researcher. Every fresh study is, therefore, a welcome addition to the existing literature.

The present study is yet another in-depth attempt to provide concrete empirical answers to a number of agrarian questions. An important feature about the study is that it addresses the whole issue of tenancy in Bengal from a broad historical perspective. The author starts by building a historical profile of the events which became responsible for the spread of share tenancy in colonial Bengal and led to the stringent and exploitative terms and conditions of this system which became typical of agrarian Bengal. As for the post-Independence period, the author examines tenancy reform measures initiated at different points of time (including those undertaken by the Left Front Government currently in power) and analyses both the NSS and field data (collected through field surveys in twelve villages in West Bengal during 1986–87) to obtain a firm understanding of the changes in tenancy structure and tenurial relations in the state.

In my view, a very strong point in the study is that considerable insights are generated, through careful analysis of primary field data, on an extremely important and hitherto unexplored issue of changing tenancy relations following the organization and political mobilization of West Bengal tenants in recent years. The programme of Operation Barga is too important to be missed by any contemporary agrarian study of West Bengal. The conclusion that, with the gaining of collective and organized strength by the tenants in West Bengal, the old tenancy relations which characterized their exploitation have started breaking up and, consequently, the prevailing system of tenancy as such does not appear to act as fetters to agrarian development, reveal a silver lining in the otherwise gloomy world of tenurial infirmities. A serious perusal of this study will throw up profound implications not only for formulating the future course of agrarian reform for the state of West Bengal, but also for other states of India where tenancy reforms have yet to make a headway.

The main features of the study are:

1. It provides empirical verification for some of the issues emanating from the theoretical debate over the institution of share tenancy. It examines the nature and role of share tenancy in Bengal as also its implications for agrarian development.
2. It summarizes and reviews the issues and debates relevant to the understanding of West Bengal agriculture, especially since Independence.
3. Unlike many earlier research attempts (particularly, the neo-classicists), the present study chooses to view the whole issue of tenancy in Bengal from its historical perspective. The study thus provides a clear understanding of the historical processes through which the tenancy system evolved in Bengal, the role it entailed for the partners in tenancy contracts and the manner in which tenancy relations were modified at different phases in history.

4. It brings out the impact of the recent phase of tenancy reforms, particularly Operation Barga, on tenurial relations in the state. In this context, the study specifically brings out changes in tenancy relations following the organization and political mobilization of the tenantry in West Bengal in recent years.

5. In order to provide a satisfactory picture of changes in tenancy system in West Bengal, the author not only draws upon old official reports (including the NSS reports) and the work of previous researchers but also has the support of extensive primary survey data which throw up contrasts of technology-tenancy minglings of two or three varieties.

6. The study bears important implications for formulating the future course of agrarian reform for the state of West Bengal. It also throws important messages for those states of India where tenancy reforms have not made much progress so far.

Altogether, the study is a sound piece of research. It is a brilliant academic attempt both for its depth of analysis and careful inter-pretation of empirical data. Dr Bhaumik's work is especially praise-worthy because it examines and repudiates many a myth concerning the agrarian world that has held sway in literature. I have no doubt that Bhaumik's comprehensive study will be warmly received by the general academic community as also the policy-makers within and outside West Bengal. Moreover, it is sure to provoke scholars to undertake similar studies in other states of India.

G.K. CHADHA
Professor of Economics
Centre for the Study of
Regional Development,
School of Social Sciences
Jawaharlal Nehru University
New Delhi

Acknowledgements

This book is an extensively revised version of my thesis accepted for the award of the Ph.D. degree by the Jawaharlal Nehru University, New Delhi. I am extremely grateful for the care and guidance of my teacher and Ph.D. supervisor, Professor G.K. Chadha of the Centre for the Study of Regional Development, Jawaharlal Nehru University. Without his deep interest in the subject and his constant encouragement, the work may not have reached its present stage. The comments by Professors V.S. Vyas, Nripen Bandyopadhyay, G.S. Bhalla and Kusum Chopra on the earlier version of this study were of great help in revision. My thanks to them all.

I am thankful to the Vice-Chancellor, Vidyasagar University, Midnapore, for sanctioning study leave and to the Indian Council of Social Science Research, New Delhi, for awarding a short-term doctoral fellowship.

I am also grateful to the anonymous referee as well as the editors at Sage Publications for their valuable suggestions.

Special thanks go to my wife, Bidisha, whose support has been extraordinary. She deserves substantial credit for anything that I have managed to accomplish.

Finally, I convey my gratitude to V. Muralidhar for providing computer facilities, often at the cost of personal convenience, and to Sadhan Sahoo for typing the manuscript.

December 1992   SANKAR KUMAR BHAUMIK

1

Introduction

Although the fact that agriculture has a crucial role to play in
general economic development needs no great elaboration, policy
analysts and administrators have engaged in debate over what
constitutes an appropriate policy for the development of agriculture
in an underdeveloped economy. Quite often, such discussion leads
to the so-called 'technology versus institution' debate. While the
technocratic solutions rely on technological packages supported by
market incentives and price supports, the institutionalists argue for
institutional reforms as an indispensable precondition for agricultural development. One need not, however, always view these as
strictly polar alternatives, particularly when it is observed that
both institutions and technology actually interact in the process of
agricultural transformation. It is possible to conceive of an 'eclectic
approach', emphasizing the need for developing the right type of
institutions alongside the technological advancement for rapid
development of agriculture. And, in this process, if a particular
institution proves 'inefficient' or poses obstacles to technical progress, suitable policies (economic and often political) have to be
devised to modify that institution or even replace it.

The present study concentrates on one important rural institution,
namely, agricultural tenancy or, more specifically, share tenancy.
Agricultural tenancy in general and share tenancy in particular
have attracted academic attention over centuries and across various
countries. The reason for this is best summed up by Byres
(1983: 32):

> sharecropping has existed since remarkably early times; has
> been extremely widespread geographically; has shown an often

astonishing historical continuity and tenacity; has, in some pre-capitalist/pre-socialist societies, such as China and Turkey, displayed a capacity to disappear and reappear. It continues to exist pervasively in the so-called Third World.

Share tenancy has aroused much controversy as regards its efficacy from economic point of view. In the late seventeenth century, the physiocrats, while studying the relative merits of *metayege* (the system of sharecropping as developed in France), considered it harmful to the advancement of agriculture (Currie, 1981: 7). Among the notable classical and neoclassical writers, Smith (1776) and Marshall (1890) also argued against the sharecropping system. Marshall considered share-rent tenancy 'inefficient' on the ground that it would act as a disincentive to the tenant as he paid the landowner a share of the produce and the tenant would employ a variable input (labour) up to the point where his share in the value of marginal product would be equal to its price (wage). Schiekele (1941) and Heady (1947) agree with Marshall and blame sharecropping for its inability to achieve a 'socially optimum allocation of resources'.

Johnson (1950), however, questioned the empirical relevance of the arguments of Marshall. Instead of accepting that sharecropping was an inefficient system, he suggested that the tenant could be induced to apply the efficient level of input by the landlord's monitoring the subsequent output, and not renewing the leases of unsatisfactory tenants. Cheung (1969) provided proof for Johnson's argument to show that share tenancy is no less efficient than the peasant-owned farming or fixed-rent tenancy.

Following the publication of Cheung's work, a number of theoretical models have been constructed by some other neoclassical economists such as Sutinen (1975), Hsiao (1975) and Lucas (1979) which go very clearly against Marshall's inefficiency argument. Nevertheless, Bardhan and Srinivasan (1971, 1974) and Jaynes (1982) raise serious objections against Cheung's formulation as well. Bardhan and Srinivasan show how sharecropping could be represented as an 'inefficient' system while assuming that the work decision is taken by the share tenant (contrary to Cheung's assumption). Bagchi (1973, 1975, 1976, 1982) criticised the models of both Cheung, and Bardhan and Srinivasan as they are based on unrealistic assumptions of competitive models.

Just as there is no unanimity of opinion among the theoretical contributors on the share tenancy–efficiency issue, a clear polarisation is also visible among the scholars conducting empirical studies. Thus, while the studies such as those of Bharadwaj (1974), Bell (1977), Hossain (1977), Jabbar (1977), Bagi (1981) and Shaban (1987) provide empirical support to the Marshallian inefficiency hypothesis, Vyas (1970), Rao (1971), Zaman (1973), Chakravarty and Rudra (1973), Dwivedi and Rudra (1973), Huang (1975), Bliss and Stern (1982), Nabi (1986) and Rudra (1992) supported Cheung's equal-efficiency argument.

While the debate on the share tenancy–efficiency issue fails to bring out a generalised opinion, it really leaves unanswered the important question as to what explains the historical perpetuation of the system of share tenancy if it is inefficient. Cheung makes an early attempt to explain the persistence of share tenancy. He writes: 'The choice of contractual arrangement is made so as to maximise the gains from risk dispersion subject to the constraints of transaction cost' (Cheung, 1969: 64). Although Cheung hinted at the risk-sharing advantages of sharecropping, it is Stiglitz (1974) who first modelled the risk-sharing advantages of sharecropping in terms of a general equilibrium model. Stiglitz also puts forward the view that the rationale for the sharecropping system lies both in its incentive effects (when direct supervision is costly or ineffective) and risk-sharing features.

Meanwhile, several other explanations have also been offered. Reid (1973, 1976, 1977) believes that the rationale for sharecropping lies in its incentives for cooperation between the landlord and the tenant to maximise the efficiency of agricultural production. Newbery (1977) argues that as rural labour markets often fail to guarantee full employment at a constant or predictable wage level, sharecropping contracts are devised to mitigate the effects of labour market uncertainty. Hallagan (1978) projects sharecropping contracts as a 'screening device' in a market where prospective tenants are endowed with different amounts of entrepreneurial ability. Under this situation, the individuals with the greatest entrepreneurial ability select to be fixed-rent tenants, those with no such ability become wage-earning workers, and the intermediate cases become share tenants. Bell (1977, 1986) and Bliss and Stern (1982), however, hold the view that sharecropping exists because of the indivisibility and imperfect marketability of some factors of production (draught animals, family labour and so on). Sharecropping enables utilization of such factors and both the landlords and tenants gain eventually. The view that sharecropping makes possible utilization of non-marketable input factors gets corroborated from the studies by Pant (1983), Nabi (1985) and Birthal and Singh (1991).

Pearce (1983), however, explains the persistence of sharecropping from the Marxian perspective. He views sharecropping as a particular method of surplus appropriation by which surplus labour is transferred to the landlord in the form of surplus product. Pearce also argues that sharecropping actually represents a transitional mode of surplus appropriation 'between forms of agrestic servitude and the full commoditization of rural labour itself' (Pearce, 1983: 45). It may persist in the early stages of capitalist development when accumulation and technical change are slow in creating developed wage-labour market, but 'there will be a tendency for such contract to be superseded by others more appropriate to high rates of accumulation in agriculture' (ibid.: 54).

Many writers have claimed that share tenancy in a backward agriculture operates not only as an isolated rural institution, but as a part of a greater, interlinked, system of rural markets (Bardhan, 1980, 1984; Basu, 1984; Ghate et al., 1992: 29–30; Otsuka et al., 1992). Very often, sharecropping contracts are found to be interlinked with credit, labour or any other contract which might have several implications for technical change and agricultural growth. Bhaduri (1973) initiated a debate on the effects of factor market interlinkages on technical progress and their implications for agrarian growth. Bhaduri shows that, in terms of a formal model, a landlord who also provides consumption loans to his tenant may have no incentive to adopt yield-increasing innovations, if the landlord's interest income from his loans to the tenant goes down. It thus provides a simple example of interlinked land-lease and credit contract constraining technical progress. Another implication of the Bhaduri model is that sharecropping in an interlocked system serves as a means of exploitation of the tenant at the hands of the landlord. It is the exploitative landlord who interlocks the land-lease and credit markets in order to extract maximum surplus from his tenants and keeps them in perpetual indebtedness, a phenomenon which Bhaduri terms 'forced commerce' (see Bhaduri, 1983: 9).

Although Bhaduri's thesis found support from Prasad (1973, 1974), Chandra (1975) and Sau (1975), it has also attracted much criticisms. Griffin (1974), Newbery (1975), Ghose and Saith (1976),

Raj (1979) and Sarap (1991) pointed out that the interlinkage of land-lease and credit contracts is rather a weak constraint for adoption of technical progress particularly in the socio-economic context of a poor village. On the contrary, they argue that if the landlord has sufficient power to exploit the tenant-borrower and to withhold the innovation, then he ought to have sufficient power to extract the extra gain from innovation by suitably manipulating the rental share, the interest rate and/or other terms and conditions of tenancy and credit contracts (also see Bell, 1991). Bardhan and Rudra (1978, 1980) observe that even in eastern India, where Bhaduri considers his model as particularly relevant, landlords quite often extend interest-free loans to the tenants, share in the cost of seeds, fertilizers and other inputs, participate in decision-making about the use of these inputs and generally take plenty of interest in productive investment on the tenant's farms. All these developments are contrary to the implications of the Bhaduri model. Further, most of the empirical studies conducted recently to examine the nature of market interlinkages also reject the idea of tenancy-credit interlinking being operative in rural areas as a means to exploit the poor tenantry (see Khasnabis and Chakraborty, 1982; Chattopadhyay and Ghosh, 1983; Taslim, 1988).

It emerges from the foregoing discussion that there have been a lot of controversies on a number of theoretical and empirical issues relating to the institution of share-crop tenancy: the efficiency of share-crop tenancy from economic point of view, its rationale for continuance along with other contractual systems, its implications for technical change and agrarian growth, and so on. These issues have attracted the attention of economists belonging to both the neoclassical and Marxist traditions. Thus, while taking cognizance of their respective standpoints on some of these issues, the present study proposes the empirical verification of some crucial aspects of share-crop tenancy with firm field data from agriculture in West Bengal. For a number of historical reasons, agriculture in West Bengal has been the best-known cradle of share-crop tenancy in India and hence the most suitable laboratory situation for observing grass-roots realities.

West Bengal has been one of the Indian states to have had a generally high pressure of population on land (with the land-man ratio declining very rapidly over time), a very high preponderance of marginal and small farmers, and a high incidence of share tenancy in Bengal. As in well-known, the colonial intervention in Bengal marked the introduction of the zamindari settlement which meant the peasants losing their customary rights over land and the zamindars becoming their proprietors. The zamindari system marked the gradual decline in the conditions of the tenants under the zamindars. Instead of providing leadership towards developments of agriculture, it embarked on subinfeudation and rack-renting. The situation worsened with the emergence of 'jotedars' in the rural scene as an influential category. The tenants were subjected to various forms of oppression and exploitation at the hands of the zamindars/jotedars. To make matters worse, there was hardly any effective initiative on the part of the colonial rulers to safeguard the interests of the tenants. The tenancy laws enacted during this period were reluctant to provide occupancy status to a large section of the share tenants. The share tenants were thus subjected to all kinds of sufferings: rent-exploitation, debt-burden, semi-feudal bondage and so on.

All the factors described above have provided rich material for research on share-crop tenancy, particularly by the economic historians. Several issues figure as the subjects of historical inquiry: How did the tenancy system evolve in Bengal under colonial rule? What were the forms of tenancy? What were the terms and conditions of tenancy contracts? What was the impact of the prevailing tenancy structure on the level of agricultural production and productivity? In fact, these are some of the issues which deserve attention if one is to appreciate fully the latter-day (post-Independence) changes in tenancy relations in Bengal brought out by a series of tenancy reform measures.

Post-Independence Bengal emerges as one of the few states in India where land reform programmes have been undertaken on a fairly large scale. Carrying forward the spirit of the Congress Agrarian Reforms Committee (1949), West Bengal went in for several measures towards the abolition, *inter alia*, of 'semi-feudal landlordism'. Intermediaries in land were abolished and subletting of land was prohibited through other reform measures in the subsequent years. A series of tenancy reform laws were enacted during the fifties, sixties and the early seventies. It is, however, a different matter that West Bengal was no exception among the states of India in its unsatisfactory implementation of many of the tenancy reform acts until about the mid-seventies. With the Left

Front Government coming to power in 1977, the situation took a dramatic turn. There was then no dearth of 'political will', so necessary for successful implementation of any reform measure pertaining to the tenants—generally the most vulnerable section in rural area. Under the Left Front regime, tenancy reforms assumed the character of an organised movement by the bargadars (share tenants). The programme Operation Barga (O.B.) was launched for the swift recording of the names of bargadars in order to secure their legal rights against rent-enhancement and eviction by the landowners. This was also accompanied by several other measures such as providing the bargadars the facility of institutional finance. The whole idea was to alter the existing power structure in the countryside through an organised movement of the bargadars in order to free them from the grip of the exploiter-landlords and village money-lenders. The tenancy reform measures as adopted by the Left Front Government, however, raise a number of empirical issues to which no satisfactory answers exist as yet: To what extent have the tenants been able to break their traditional tenurial relationships in the aftermath of their political mobilization for an organized struggle (as through Operation Barga) in the state? To what extent have the tenants been successful in resetting the terms and conditions of tenancy contracts in their own favour following O.B.? What contribution does the programme make in terms of improving the allocation efficiency of resources by the tenants? What has been the impact of O.B. on the level of agricultural productivity and production?

It is to be noted that apart from adopting various tenancy reform measures, West Bengal agriculture underwent some structural changes during the post-Independence period. There has been a gradual increase in net sown area, not leaving much scope for further expansion. The increase in cropping intensity is also noticeable, although it still hovered around a low level of 1.35 during 1984–87 (see Appendix Table A1). The most significant change has occurred in respect of the cropping pattern, particularly in recent years with the emergence of crops such as rice (Boro) and wheat which are almost fully irrigated and cultivated with high-yielding seeds (see Appendix Table A2). The increase in the proportion of cropped area under some commercial crops (such as jute, potatoes and oilseeds) has also been appreciable. Another important aspect of agriculture in West Bengal has been that it has now come out of its pre-Independence stagnation. Almost all the important crops have registered positive growth rates in terms of area, yield and production during the period 1957–58 to 1986–87 (see Appendix Table A3). The most significant performance has been recorded in case of rice (Boro), wheat, potatoes and oilseeds. It is, of course, true that the growth has not been uniform all through the period. While crops such as rice (Boro), wheat and potatoes performed quite impressively during the sub-period 1967–68 to 1976–77, there are some other crops 'rice (Aman), oilseeds and jute', which recorded better growth rates in yield and production during 1977–78 to 1986–87. It is a significant achievement that the growth rates in yield and production are positive for all sub-periods in the case of total foodgrains in the face of a decline in the growth rate of area cropped (Appendix Table A3).

On the technological front too, West Bengal agriculture achieved some progress although it may not appear very impressive when compared with other green revolution areas in India. The technological breakthrough in West Bengal agriculture comes through greater use of biochemical rather than mechanical inputs (see Appendix Table A4). There has been some progress in the percentage of net sown area irrigated although it stands at a somewhat lower level of 34.25 per cent in 1982–83. Besides the increase in the per hectare consumption of fertilizer, the percentage of cropped area using high-yielding seeds has witnessed a steady increase. Similarly, some progress in agricultural infrastructure can be observed, particularly, for example, in terms of the percentage of villages electrified, the number of regulated markets per million of rural population. There is also some evidence of the expansion of the network of commercial banks in rural areas. While all these aspects indicate the changing character of agriculture in West Bengal, to what extent and in what manner these changes have affected the tenancy structure is also an important area of research.

Thus, West Bengal offers a suitable area for the empirically verification for some of the issues emanating from the theoretical debate over the institution of tenancy as also for the examination of the changing character of tenancy at different phases in history. It is to be admitted that no study on tenancy with reference to Bengal would be complete unless it brings in the aspects of changing tenancy relations consequent to colonial intervention, post-Independence tenancy reforms accompanied by organized struggles of the tenants and also the technological improvements in recent years. It goes without saying that it may be difficult to incorporate all these issues in a single study since each one of them deserves to form the subject of a detailed inquiry in its own right. Nevertheless, we have attempted in the present study to touch upon all these aspects, to the extent possible, by placing the whole issue of tenancy in Bengal in its broad historical perspective (unlike the procedure usually followed by neoclassical scholars). This study thus provides a clear understanding of the historical processes through which the tenancy system evolved itself in Bengal, the role it entailed for the partners in tenancy contracts and the manner in which tenancy relations were modified at different phases in history. We also believe that it is through an understanding of the changing character of tenancy relations at different historical phases that we may conjecture upon the future pattern of tenancy in the state.

2

Tenancy Structure in Pre-Independence Bengal

The **main purpose** of this chapter is to provide a brief introduction on the tenancy situation in pre-Independence Bengal. Specifically, our objective is to see how the system of tenancy (particularly, share tenancy) evolved in Bengal. Some ideas about the extent of tenant cultivation and the terms and conditions of tenancy contracts around or a little before the dawn of Independence may also be clarified.

Evolution of the Tenancy System

To understand the evolution as well as the changing structure of tenancy in pre-Independence Bengal[1], it may be best to begin with a description of the agrarian structure that prevailed in pre-British Bengal, in order to understand the subsequent changes brought about by British intervention. Contemporary historians differ sharply on the nature of agrarian structure in pre-colonial Bengal.[2] The relatively more influential school of opinion describes it as being, like the agrarian economies in many other parts of India, 'self-subsisting and self-perpetuating in character' (see Chowdhury, 1967: 258; Thorner, 1962: 51). In a self-subsisting economy, peasant farming was the norm and production was carried out mainly to fulfil consumption needs. There existed a kind of harmony between

---

[1] Pre-Independence Bengal means undivided Bengal comprising the present-day Bangladesh and West Bengal (India).

[2] For a summarised view of the contrasting opinions on the question of agrarian structure in pre-British Bengal, see Chaudhuri (1982: 86–87); Government of Bengal (1940: 8–11); and Dasgupta (1984: 3–34).

agriculture and the handicraft industry. Although the land undisputedly belonged to the original cultivators, the question of formal property rights over land did not arise since land was available in abundance (Habib, 1982: 54). In other words, the individual holdings were seen more in terms of *possession* than *ownership* as they were cultivated primarily for subsistence by the self-cultivating and possessing types of cultivators. This means that there was little scope for the development of relationships between landlords, sharecroppers and agricultural labourers and a kind of cohesiveness centering around agriculture did exist in Bengal (see Mukherjee, 1957: 14–27; Patel, 1952: 9–10, 32–33).

The Moghal period was marked by several changes in the system of assessment and the collection of revenue. Nevertheless, an important agrarian feature of the time was that the peasants continued to enjoy the customary rights over the land occupied by them. Generally, there were two types of cultivators at that time— the *khudkasht* ryots who enjoyed undisturbed possession of their holdings subject to the payment of their dues and the *paikasht* ryots who were non-residential cultivators and had come into the village to cultivate temporarily and thus enjoyed no security of tenure (Government of Bengal, 1940: 11). During this period, the revenue demand of the state varied between a half to a third of the gross produce and, as far as possible, the settlement of revenue was made directly with the cultivators. The task of revenue collection was assigned to a class of agents called 'zamindars' (Sinha; 1968: 2), and they often performed this function hereditarily. Another important feature of agrarian relations of this period was that the cultivator could not ordinarily be evicted from land unless he failed to pay the stipulated revenue to the zamindar (Sen, 1962: 55–56; Sinha, 1968: 9). The sale of land was a very rare phenomenon.

With the arrival of the East India Company, the agrarian structure of Bengal underwent a radical change. The Company purchased the *talukdari* rights (that is, the rights of revenue collection from the peasants) over the three estates of Calcutta, Gobindapur and Sutanuti in 1698 and obtained the Diwani of Bengal, Bihar and Orissa in 1765. Since then, the Company experimented with several changes in the method of revenue collection with the sole objective of maximizing its earnings. It introduced the quinquennial settlement (1772), the decennial settlement (1789) and the Revenue Farm Contracts on a five-yearly basis whereby the revenue-collecting rights were distributed through auction to the highest bidders. All these, however, ended in extreme rack-renting, often in the forcible collection of revenue, and consequently placed an unbearable burden on the cultivating peasantry[3]. The situation was aggravated with the great Bengal famine of 1770 which wiped out nearly 35 per cent of the total and 50 per cent of the agricultural population, besides rendering a third of the cultivable land as waste. This was followed by the famines in 1784, 1787 and 1790, which further increased the oppression and misery of the cultivating peasants. The foregoing developments, *inter alia*, led to peasant resistance which was expressed in terms of the Fakir and Sanyasi rebellions of 1772–89 (Sen, 1962: 58).

The prevailing agrarian situation urgently called for a settlement which would both rehabilitate agriculture and stabilise revenue collection. Thus the Permanent Settlement was introduced in 1793 under the governorship of Lord Cornwallis. Under this Settlement, the zamindars, who were the erstwhile collectors of revenue, were declared the proprietors of land in exchange for the payment of revenue fixed in perpetuity. While introducing the Permanent Settlement, Cornwallis visualized both a steady collection of revenue and the restoration of confidence among the zamindars necessary for them to undertake the capital investment needed for arresting the recent decline in agricultural output.[4]

History has shown that while the first objective of Cornwallis was fulfilled, the second was not. The emergence of zamindari system by itself did not promote capital investment by the existing zamindars (Government of India, 1976: 3–4). Rather, as land became a saleable commodity, the estates of many zamindars were sold for arrears of revenue, the new purchasers being the persons working under the old zamindars, merchants, money-lenders,

[3] It has been found in one estimate that between 1765 and 1793, the amount of revenue nearly doubled. See Chaudhuri (1975a: 2).

[4] See Chaudhuri (1982: 88). It has been argued by many scholars that the Company's motive behind the introduction of the Permanent Settlement was confined not only to a secure collection of revenue but also to create an ally among the people of this country which would have identical interest and unquestioned loyalty to the colonial rule. It has also been argued that by establishing a secure and permanent individual ownership over land, the colonial rulers could successfully divert the interests of the contemporary moneyed class into land in lieu of industrial entrepreneurship. See Mukherjee (1957: 52); Dutt (1979: 232); Ghosh and Dutt (1977: 4); Bettelheim (1977: 20).

traders and the middle class in urban areas (Sen, 1979: 7). These new 'intruders' were interested only in squeezing high rent out of land. They often delegated the collection of rent on to the middlemen (Thorner, 1962: 54). Even the surviving zamindars, instead of managing their estates directly and undertaking the responsibility of improving the conditions of agriculture, as was expected of them, embarked on a system of subinfeudation. The process of subinfeudation extended to a long hierarchy of sub-tenants, called *dar-patnis, dar-izaras* and even further subordinate tenures. Even where there was no subinfeudation, the peasants were rack-rented by the local officials and the *naibs* became *de facto* zamindars who imposed innumerable illegal exactions or *awabs* on them.[5] Under the increasing burden of rent, *awabs* and other extractions the cultivating peasantry was obviously left with very few means to go in for agricultural improvement.

For nearly seven decades since 1793, the government was primarily concerned with safeguarding its revenue. This was the background to all the legislation passed during this period, including 'Haptam' (Regulation VII of 1799) which vested unrestricted powers in the zamindars for seizing the crops and other personal property of the cultivators, even arresting them, in order to realize rent arrears. This unrestricted power of the zamindars coupled with complete denial of the customary rights of the cultivators created conditions of growing unrest among the cultivating peasantry in this period.[6]

Thus the government which had so far continued with its policy of neutrality was compelled to formulate the first tenancy legislation—the Rent Act of 1859—so as to improve the relation between the landlords and their tenants (Chowdhury, 1967: 308). The declared aim of the Act was to strengthen the position of the ryots through a clearer definition of their rights on the one hand, and by placing restrictions on the landlord's powers to effect rent enhancement and eviction on the other (Ghosh and Dutt, 1977: 20–21).

---

[5] According to one estimate, sometime in the 1930s in the district of Bakarganj the amount collected annually over and above legal rents was Rs 20 lakh, which was more than the entire government revenue for the district. See Government of Bengal (1941: 34).

[6] It may be noted that this period marked the great Santal insurrection in Bengal (1855–56), the first organized peasant movement against the oppression of landlord-money-lenders and traders. See Government of West Bengal (1980).

The Rent Act of 1859 demarcated three groups among the ryots based on the duration of their tenantry (Sen, 1982: 10–13): (*a*) *mukuraridars* or *istamraridars* who cultivated land at fixed rate since the time of the Permanent Settlement or the ryots for whom rent had not been changed for twenty years; (*b*) occupancy ryots who had cultivated land for an uninterrupted period of twelve years; and (*c*) non-occupancy ryots who could not prove twelve years' uninterrupted possession over land. The Act provided some security and protection to the occupancy ryots against rent enhancement and eviction. For example, the Act declared that the rent could be enhanced only if it was below the 'prevailing rate' paid by the same class of ryots for land of a similar description or if the value of the produce had increased in the meantime. The non-occupancy ryots were given no security either against rent enhancement or eviction. The unprotected non-occupancy ryots were thus left to obey the dictates of the landlords.

By providing occupancy right to only a section of the peasantry, the Rent Act of 1859 tried to separate them from the large section of non-occupancy ryots (Ghosh and Dutt, 1977: 22). Moreover, with the obvious vagueness of the term 'prevailing rate' in the determination of rent and in the absence of village records, the difficulty in proving possession of land for twelve continuous years, the ryots continued to be subjected to rack-renting insecurity of tenure. This resulted in agrarian struggles such as the Pabna disturbances (1873), which forced fresh legislation governing landlord-tenant relations.

The Bengal Tenancy Act of 1885 was passed with the objective of consolidating the enactments of the earlier Acts. It stipulated that any ryot who had been in possession of any land for twelve years, either by himself or through inheritance, would become a settled ryot of the village with occupancy rights in the land he already possessed and would immediately acquire those rights in any new land which he took for cultivation. The Act also puts restrictions on the arbitrary enhancement of rents and provided that no ejection was permissible without a decree from the civil court. An important aspect of the Act was that by introducing the sale and purchase of the property cultivated by the occupancy ryots (subject to the payment of a portion of sale proceeds as landlord's fee), it introduced rapid changes in the tenancy strata in Bengal. The rent of the non-occupancy ryots, however, was left to be fixed through an agreement between the two parties. Unlike occupancy ryots, they were liable to be evicted and did not enjoy the other conventional rights allowed to the occupancy ryots.

The extremely vulnerable position of the non-occupancy tenants was thus the agrarian reality of the times. From this it may not be concluded that the rest of the peasantry was free of agrarian handicaps. For example, for no section of the peasantry including the occupancy tenants, was an effective limit put to subinfeudation, subletting was not banned, and under certain conditions even occupancy ryots could be evicted and the zamindar had the right of resumption. Thus, in effective terms, the Bengal Tenancy Act of 1885 could do very little towards altering the prevailing agrarian structure. The situation was still one of lack of enterprise on the part of the zamindars, continuing exploitation of actual cultivators, and a prolonged backwardness of Bengal agriculture.[7]

The period between 1928 and 1940 witnessed several further amendments to the provisions of the Bengal Tenancy Act, the most important being the Tenancy Act Amendment Bill (1928). Its main purpose was, as one commentator puts it, to strike 'a delicate balance between the interests of landlords, tenants and undertenants' (Chatterjee, 1984: 4). As regards the bargadars or sharecroppers (who had been included in the category of non-occupancy ryots all along), the draft Bill based on the recommendations of the John Kerr Committee (1923) declared that the produce-paying cultivators who supplied their own seeds and cattle and produced crops of their own choice, could be treated as tenants. However, amidst opposition from the landholders, the government did not implement the proposal and merely declared that sharecroppers who paid a fixed *proportion* of produce were not occupancy tenants but those who paid a fixed *quantity* of produce would obtain such status. Regarding the under-ryots, the Bill did not provide any safeguard except that rent could not exceed the amount paid by their superior ryots by 25 per cent and they would have the right to claim recognition as occupancy ryot on the payment of a *salami* when their superior ryots abandoned

---

[7] It has been found that between 1891–1901 foodgrains output had declined at the yearly rate of 0.04 per cent while the rate of decline increased to 1.28 per cent if considered for the period 1896–1906. Between 1870–90, there were thirteen years when two or more divisions of Bengal reported a shortfall of 15 per cent or more from the normal level of rice production. See Sen (1982: 46).

their holdings. The under-ryots could be evicted by their superior landlords if they wanted the land for self-cultivation.

What emerges from the foregoing discussion is that the colonial land policy while establishing formal property rights over land also conceived of a variety of tenancy legislation which claimed to protect small-peasant production in Bengal. This dual stance points to the conceptual contradictions in the land policy (*ibid.*: 8), which ultimately accentuated the process of subinfeudation and the extensive rent exploitation of the cultivating peasantry in Bengal. To this system of land tenure may be added the disincentives against the entry of domestic savings into native industrial enterprises and the destruction of indigenous manufacturing to complete the story of economic deprivation inflicted by the colonial rule. In any case, on the domestic agrarian scene, there emerged a class of rent-receivers, usurers and petty traders who were totally divorced from land and entirely uninterested in the conditions of social production. These people were only concerned with distribution of the surplus without having any role in its creation (*ibid.*: 13).

Jotedars and the Spread of Sharecropping

Under colonial rule, there emerged along with the zamindars as the proprietors of land, a new category of large landowners in Bengal, commonly called *jotedars*, who took to subletting and extracting heavy rent from the tenants. In fact, much of the expansion of the sharecropping tenancy in Bengal owed itself to the growth of the jotedari- system. The Buchanan–Hamilton Report clearly indicated how, after the Permanent Settlement, there took place a phenomenal growth of jotedars in the Dinajpur and Rangpur districts of Bengal (Sen, 1979: 9). It has been stated that one of about every sixteen farmers was a jotedar who would rent land ranging between 30 and 100 acres, self-cultivate a portion thereof while the remaining (often much bigger portion) would be leased out on a sharecropping basis. The jotedars came mostly from the erstwhile class of traders and rich farmers. Throughout the nineteenth century, the jotedars played an important role in land reclamation in some areas, particularly in the North Bengal districts and some parts of the 24-Parganas and Khulna districts (Bose, 1982: 11–18; Bandyopadhyay, 1975: 9; Bandyopadhyay, 1977:

A113). In some areas, the expenses of reclamation were initially borne by the jotedars but such lands were later turned to share-crop cultivation (Sen, 1972: 6). In other areas, the tribals were given land to clear jungles and settle for cultivation. However, after a few years, they were either evicted from the land or resettled on the same land as bargadars.

In Bengal, there also emerged a class of 'bhadralok jotedars' under British rule. This comprised brahmins, kayasthas, other upper-caste people, mukhtars, pleaders, judges, magistrates, doctors, and so on. These people purchased land rights and threw up such lands into barga cultivation since that provided a safe and profitable investment of their savings (*ibid.*: 3). The spread of these jotedars is very well documented by the various Bengal district Gazetteers for the first decade of the twentieth century (see Sen, 1979: 11).

The spread of sharecropping in Bengal was also due to several other factors. First, with the destruction of indigenous manufacturing, a vast population was thrown back into agriculture and had to rely on barga cultivation for survival (Sen, 1982). Second, with the diminution of the peasant holdings due, *inter alia*, to the operation of inheritance laws, many peasants started depending on barga cultivation to supplement their income. Third, the 'bhadralok' would not involve himself in actual cultivation since in terms of the prevailing socio-cultural milieu, this would erode his social status. Indeed, the inhibitions and taboos against physical participation in agriculture were too strong for the upper-caste rent-receiving 'bhadralok' of times (Chaudhury, 1967: 320; Bandyopadhyay; 1975: 9). Fourth, the growth of barga cultivation owed to the creation of urban job opportunities for the more educated middle class landholding families.

It has been argued by recent historians that the spread of the barga system in Bengal owed a great deal to the process of 'depeasantization' which started first with the famines and was later accelerated with the emergence of grain merchants and big farmers as creditors in the countryside (Chaudhuri, 1975b: 128–45). Thus ensued large-scale sale and transfer of peasant holdings (*ibid.*: 137–38). However, the moot point is that the expropriation of peasant holdings, instead of giving impetus to capitalist development of agriculture led to a fast expansion of share-crop tenancy (Ghosh and Dutt, 1977: 79).

The situation took a serious turn since the 1930s as the pressure of population on land had assumed acute proportions leading to a sharp decline in the land-man ratio.[8] This was accompanied by the depression of 1929–30 which added further to the sufferings of the poor peasantry. Prior to the period of depression, with the rise in the prices of agricultural commodities, the landowners rushed to convert their tenancies into sharecropping to augment the level of their earnings. The post-depression period witnessed, on the one hand, the destruction of rural artisans and, on the other, further sales and transfers of peasant holdings for failure to repay debts (Cooper, 1988: 38–39). These people had no other alternative but to queue up to be absorbed in the army of bargadars. Furthermore, the Tenancy Act Amendment Bill (1928), by disallowing the bargadars to acquire occupancy rights, encouraged the landowners during this period to put their land to barga cultivation. Thus, even during the period of the depression, when agricultural prices were declining, the landowners preferred leasing out their lands on barga because that involved no risk of losing lands to the bargadars. Finally, the Bengal Famine of 1943 also resulted in large-scale land alienation and conversion of owner-cultivators into bargadars (*ibid.*: 53–57).

We have mentioned the various reasons for the spread of share-cropping in Bengal. However, our discussion so far has left several other questions unanswered: Why did the non-cultivating land-owners prefer sharecropping instead of cultivation of their land through wage labour? Why did the poor peasants take up share-cropping instead of wage employment? Why was sharecropping, rather than fixed rent tenancy, the dominant form of tenancy?

It may be argued that sharecropping provided the landowners with the easiest and cheapest methods of maximizing their earnings from land as it required very little time for supervision (Chaudhuri, 1975b: 153). Further, in a situation of labour shortage or threatened labour scarcity, the share-contract was preferred to cultivation with wage labour (Cooper, 1988: 59). Moreover, if the landowners also acted as creditors and/or grain traders, which in very many cases they did, the preference was for sharecropping as it assured them of a rental income which was larger than the one derived from direct

---

[8] The change in the land-man ratio occurred with the decline in death rate and the almost complete exhaustion of the possibility of further increase in cultivable area. See *Census of India* (1951: 373).

cultivation (Chaudhuri, 1975*b*: 152). The creditor-landowners could thus overcome the problem of supervision, which became intractable, particularly when their newly acquired holdings were scattered. By offering their plots for sharecropping, they could ensure positive earnings from money-lending since the loans were mostly repaid in the form of grain after harvest.

As for the poor peasants, the preference was for sharecropping rather than wage employment even when this meant smaller net earnings. This is because sharecropping provided them relative independence along with the guarantee of greater and more assured employment over the year (*ibid.*: 160). The sharecroppers also enjoyed higher social status compared with the agricultural labourers. Moreover, most of the sharecroppers were erstwhile cultivators who were dispossessed of their land (fully or partly) after the occurrence of famine/epidemic or due to failure to repay the debts or were tribals evicted from areas brought under cultivation (Dasgupta, 1984*b*: 43). Naturally, these people preferred to continue cultivation, even on sharecropping terms, of the very plots they had been cultivating for long.

As regards the landowners' preference for sharecropping rather than fixed-rent tenancy, several explanations could be put forward: first, the variety of tenancy legislation which sought to provide occupancy rights to the tenants paying fixed rent (in cash or kind) induced the landowners to convert their tenancy arrangements to sharecropping. Second, the share accruing under crop-sharing basis was much larger than that which obtained under fixed rent contracts.[9] Third, the landowners' preference for crop-sharing tenancy could be due to their motive for risk-sharing. This was so because this system was relatively more widespread in the western part of Bengal which was more vulnerable to both drought and

[9] It has been reported in the Survey and Settlement Report for the district of Nadia (1918–26) that half the produce under crop-sharing arrangement was equal to Rs. 4 per bigha of land compared to the cash rent of ryots at Rs. 2–7–10. The Survey and Settlement reports for the districts of Bogra and Pabna also noted that the sharecroppers paid on average twice as much as the lowest category of ryots paying cash rents (referred by Cooper, 1983: 233). The Land Revenue Commission (1938) also noted that sharecropping 'provides a very simple way of raising rents without recourse to courts, for instead of getting a fixed rent which may be three, four, five or even as much as seven rupees per acre he will be getting half of a crop which may be worth as much as forty rupees per acre'. See Government of Bengal (1941: 47–48).

floods, rather than in eastern Bengal where rainfall was heavier and the harvest more assured (*ibid.*). Fourthly, the sharp rise in foodgrain prices made it more lucrative on the part of the landowner to receive rent in kind. The fact that many of the new owners of land were also traders in foodgrains or jute even led to the substitution of cash-paying tenancies and under-tenancies into produce-paying ones in many districts of Bengal since the 1920s (Chatterjee, 1982: 172).

Terms and Conditions of Tenancy Contracts

The terms and conditions of tenancy contracts varied, depending upon the type of arrangements made between the two parties (Sen, 1962: 116–17). For example, the *sanja* tenants were required to pay a fixed quantity of produce as rent. The Bengal Tenancy Act (1885) sought to protect from eviction the *sanja* tenants who made written arrangements with their landowners. The *utbandi* tenants were tenants-at-will and were always at the mercy of the proprietors. The *gulo* tenants enjoyed no security of tenure either; their rents were determined in terms of a portion of the produce but the payments were to be made in cash. Under the *krishani* system the landowner provided everything except labour and the tenant obtained his wage in kind, in terms of a proportion (generally a third) of the produce. The *krishani* was often bonded by debt-obligation to the landowner which he had little chance to repay in his life-time, leaving him practically in semi-feudal bondage. A variant of the *krishani* system was found in some parts of the northern districts of Bengal where the tenants were not necessarily indebted to their landlords and the very laborious nature of work and labour scarcity tilted the tenancy arrangements in favour of the tenants and they were allowed to retain a half of the produce (Dasgupta, 1984*b*: A4). These features apart, in a majority of the cases, the tenants were responsible both for labour and other operational decisions such as those for crop-patterns and input use.

The sharing of crop under share tenancy was mostly done on the principle of equal shares (Government of Bengal, 1941: 47). However, deviation from the principle of equal-sharing was not uncommon where the land was more fertile or the landowner provided the seed (Cooper, 1983: 233). In some cases, the landowners made arbitrary deductions before the crop was shared. In view of the aforementioned facts, it is clear that the actual share belonging to the sharecropper was almost always less than half the produce; it was anything between a third and half of the produce (Dasgupta, 1948*b*).

In the matter of sharing of input costs, the general practice was to expect the sharecropper to contribute practically everything—his own seeds, manure, plough and cattle. However, if the landowner contributed some inputs that affected the equal-sharing rule (Cooper, 1983). The place of threshing was customarily decided by the landowner while the operational decisions regarding cultivation were taken by the sharecroppers.

It has been reported that the sharecropping contracts often led to a kind of dependency relationship between the sharecropper and his landlord (*ibid.*: 237–38). The power of the landlord, by virtue of his tight control over land, enabled him to extract *begar* (free labour) from the sharecropper's family. Although *begar* could be enforced at any time, it guaranteed the supply of labour to the landowner, particularly at the crucial time of the year when the need and, consequently, the demand for labour was the highest. That would also be the time when the wage rate would ordinarily be higher. In any case, the extent of *begar* depended upon whether the landowner lived in the locality and whether he had *khas* land for self-cultivation or whether the sharecropper lived on the land provided by him (*ibid.*).

The most crucial aspect of the dependency relationship was the indebtedness of the sharecroppers. In cases where the landowners acted as creditors, the debt bondage of the sharecroppers reinforced the dependency relationship between them (ibid.: 240–43). The usual practice was to take loans in grain from the landowners a few months before the harvest and repay one and half times the amount after the harvest. In the case of seed loans, the rate of interest charged was 100 per cent. The interest rose further with the failure of the borrowing peasants to pay off the loan in time (Chaudhuri, 1969: 32–33). If the landowner happened to be the trader, loan transactions enabled him to seize the crops of the sharecroppers. It has been observed that the debt obligation of the sharecropper very often exceeded the total value of his produce and quite naturally, this threw him further down into the debt trap inasmuch as he could not make do without contracting a fresh loan, first, for continuing the cycle of production and, second, for household consumption. Thus, it was the strikingly exploitative content of the sharecropping system that lent full impetus for the campaign of the Kisan Sabha in Bengal for debt-suspension in the 1930s and 1940s.

The Extent of Share-crop Tenancy

We have so far discussed in general terms the changes in land policy, the steady expansion of sharecropping tenancy and the terms and conditions of sharecropping contracts in Bengal under colonial rule. It would also be worthwhile for our purpose to understand in quantitative terms the extent of barga (sharecropping) cultivation in colonial Bengal. It is, of course, not very easy to provide a precise estimate of land under barga cultivation or the change in the percentage of area held by the bargadars, particularly when the available data on barga cultivation were not fully satisfactory and could scarcely provide any basis for firm conclusion. Although data relating to the extent of barga cultivation became available since the conduct of survey and settlement operations in various districts of Bengal in the early decades of this century, data for the whole of Bengal were not available until the time of the Land Revenue Commission (1938).

The Land Revenue Commission conducted special inquiries in a number of villages in each district to ascertain the extent of barga cultivation as also the proportion of agricultural families dependent on the barga system as their main means of livelihood. The data gathered, however, suffer from the problem of underestimation, partly because of hesitation and concealment by the officials (Kanungos) entrusted with the job and partly because of ambiguity in the definition of bargadars (Cooper, 1988: 306–7). Nevertheless, one may use the data to obtain a broad idea of the extent of barga cultivation in the Bengal districts in the 1930s.

Table 2.1 provides data on the proportion of agricultural families living (mainly/entirely) as bargadars, as well as the proportion of agricultural land cultivated by them in various districts of Bengal. The important point to note is that quite a substantial proportion

Table 2.1
Extent of Barga Cultivation in the Districts of Bengal (1938)

District	Proportion of	
	Agricultural families living as bargadars	Area cultivated by bargadars
Jessore	4.2	22.1
Khulna	13.2	50.2
Dacca	6.9	22.9
Mymensingh	7.3	10.3
Faridpur	23.8	11.4
Bakarganj	7.1	44.7
Chittagong	1.8	11.9
Tippera	1.1	12.4
Noakhali	2.2	16.8
Rajshahi	13.0	15.0
Rangpur	19.1	22.8
Bogra	13.4	16.0
Pabna	26.1	19.4
Burdwan	27.2	25.2
Birbhum	12.9	24.8
Bankura	6.6	29.2
Midnapore	6.5	17.1
Hoogly	27.7	30.5
Howrah	27.1	23.4
24-Parganas	18.7	22.3
Nadia	6.7	24.1
Murshidabad	10.9	25.8
Dinajpur	13.8	14.5
Jalpaiguri	26.6	25.9
Malda	18.7	9.6
Bengal	**12.2**	**21.1**

Source: *Report of the Land Revenue Commission Bengal*, Vol. II, 1940, pp. 117, 118–19.

of agricultural land was under barga cultivation in almost all the districts of Bengal. For Bengal as a whole, 21.1 per cent of agricultural land was estimated to be barga land. Another point to note is that the proportion of families living as bargadars as well as the proportion of land cultivated by them were both decidedly higher in West Bengal districts as compared to East Bengal if Khulna and Bakarganj districts, where the extent of barga cultivation was reported to be exceptionally high, are excluded. The share of West

Bengal would go up further if one takes into account the problem of underestimation of the barga system, particularly in the districts of Bankura, Midnapore, Nadia and Murshidabad.[10] In any case, a large tract of land, possibly around one-fourth, was under barga cultivation in West Bengal by the end of the 1930s.

The Tenancy System and Agricultural Growth

We have seen how the colonial land policy in Bengal led to the emergence of a class of people called zamindars as the proprietors of land. The zamindars lived their life in complete dissociation from the day-to-day affairs of agriculture and even handed over the task of revenue collection to an army of intermediaries. The cultivating peasantry had to bear a tremendous burden of rent and illegal exactions by these intermediaries and was left with very few means for agricultural improvement. Further, with the emergence of the jotedars, a class of rich peasants, there was an alienation of peasant holdings. The important point here is that in the case of Bengal, the so-called rich peasants, instead of taking to cultivation along capitalist lines, utilized their resources in money-lending and/or in acquiring the alienated holdings of the peasants and sub-letting them on sharecropping basis.

The sharecropping system, however, acted as a 'built-in depressor' in Bengal's agriculture (Thorner, 1962: 57). This is because very often the sharecroppers were too poor to pay for improved methods of cultivation and the jotedars showed no inclination to take to capitalist farming. Moreover, while under the sharecropping arrangement, the process of production was carried out by the sharecropper with his extremely limited resource-base, he had to surrender a large part of the gross produce to the jotedars (Chaudhuri, 1975b: 161). Added to this, there was further disincentive to improved methods of cultivation under the constant threat of eviction (Sen, 1972: 13). In sum, the whole arrangement of sharecropping in pre-Independence Bengal was not conducive to the adoption of improved

[10] The Report of the Land Revenue Commission admitted that in the districts of Bankura and Midnapore, *sanja* tenants who usually paid fixed produce or fixed produce-cum-cash rent were excluded from the definition of bargadars. In Nadia and Murshidabad, *utbandi* and *faslijama*, which meant fixed produce-rent paying tenancies, were also excluded.

methods of cultivation. Given the numerical preponderance of sharecroppers, agriculture suffered an all round setback.[11]

To sum up, under the land policy adopted by the colonial rulers in Bengal, the peasants lost their customary rights over land and the zamindars, the erstwhile collectors of revenue, became the owners of land. The zamindari system, however, instead of promoting large-scale investment in agriculture led to the growth of sub-infeudation and rack-renting of the cultivating peasantry. The peasants were subjected to exploitation in various forms and were left with very little means to go in for agricultural improvements. Alongside the zamindars, there emerged a class of rich peasants in Bengal, called the 'jotedars', whose main purpose was not to take to cultivation on capitalist lines but to augment the level of their earnings by investing the extracted surplus in money-lending or purchasing the alienated holdings of the peasants and turning them into barga cultivation. Apart from the spread of jotedari system, the growth of sharecropping in Bengal owed to several other factors: among them, increasing pressure of population on land with the destruction of indigenous manufacturing, the process of depeasant-ization under famines or debt-burden, the creation of urban job opportunities for a section of landowners, upper class/caste inhibi-tions and taboos against physical participation in agriculture, the Depression of the 1930s, the passing of tenancy legislation giving occupancy rights to the tenants who paid fixed rent but refusing the same to sharecroppers. As for the landowners, an additional incen-tive was that sharecropping, while requiring very little time for direct

---

[11] In the well-known study conducted by Blyn for the period 1891–1947, it has been found that the annual average growth of yield as well as output were negative (−0.55 per cent and −0.73 per cent respectively) for foodgrains in Greater Bengal (which includes West Bengal, present-day Bangladesh, Bihar and Orissa) while the growth rate of population was 0.65 per cent. As regards agricultural technology, Blyn's study shows that the percentage of irrigated land to net cultivated land was 13.3 per cent during 1908/09–1921/22 which increased marginally to 15.0 per cent during 1922/23–1945/46. Similarly, the progress on the front of cropping intensity was found to be very low. For example, the proportion of double cropped area to net sown area which was 20.0 per cent during 1891/92–1918/19 increased only to 21.4 per cent during 1919/20–1945/46. Further, a very small percentage of total cropped area was under improved seed (6.2 per cent only in 1938/39). All these facts clearly indicate the stagnation in agricultural technology and production in Bengal during the closing 50 years or so of the British rule. For details, see Blyn (1966: Chapters 5–8).

supervision, provided an earning from land which exceeded the earnings from cultivation through wage labour. The terms and conditions of sharecropping contracts varied depending upon the arrangements agreed upon between the landowners and the tenants. The share of output going to the tenants varied between a third and half and the input costs were mostly borne by the share tenants. The sharecropping contracts often led to a kind of 'dependency relationship' whereby the landowners obtained 'begar' from the sharecroppers by virtue of their control over land and such relationships were reinforced where they also supplied credit to the sharecroppers. It was an arrangement where the tenants had neither the means nor any incentive to venture into agricultural improvements and this contributed to the backwardness of agriculture in colonial Bengal.

3

Tenancy Reforms and Changing Tenancy Structure in Post-Independence Bengal

In the last chapter we discussed the tenancy situation in pre-Independence Bengal. We noted how the colonial land policy led to the emergence of share tenancy in Bengal. The vast majority of the sharecroppers under the colonial rule enjoyed practically no security of tenure. In fact, they were subjected to various forms of oppression and exploitation at the hands of landowners/jotedars. To make matters worse, there was hardly any effective initiative on the part of the colonial rulers to safeguard their interests. The tenancy laws enacted during this period were reluctant to provide occupancy status to them. Only with the formation of the All India Kisan Sabha in 1936 did the interests of the sharecroppers in their struggle against the colonial rule and rural vested interests start getting adequate attention. This contributed to a large extent in shaping some of the recommendations of the Land Revenue Commission (1938).[1] Nothing concrete, however, came the way of the sharecroppers. Even in the post-Independence period, Bengal did not witness a noticeable improvement in the conditions of the sharecroppers for quite a few years. There was hesitation at the political level as regards giving them adequate security against eviction by the landowners. Furthermore, even the tenancy laws enacted during the initial period were hardly put into actual effect. This along with the usual loopholes in the Acts led to all kinds of suffering—such as, eviction, rent-exploitation, the debt-burden.

The situation changed effectively with the left-wing political

---

[1] The two main recommendations of the Commission were that: (a) the bargadars be declared tenants although they might not have all the rights of occupancy, and (b) the share of the crop legally recoverable from the bargadars should be one-third, instead of half. See Government of Bengal (1940: 253).

parties coming into power. It was a great historical development that the sharecroppers along with the other weaker sections of the agricultural population could be mobilised to wage a struggle against all rural vested interests. And with this, Bengal witnessed the coming into power of Left Coalition Governments, first for two brief periods between 1967 and 1970, and then the Left Front Government continuously from 1977 onwards. With the gaining of political power by the left parties, the land policy was given serious attention so as to safeguard the interest of the weaker sections in the countryside, which included the sharecroppers. Thus we may witness two distinct phases as regards the adoption and implementation of tenancy reform measures in post-Independence Bengal. The first phase extends from 1947 to 1977 (excluding the years of Left Coalition Governments during 1967–70) and the second phase is the period since 1977, that is, since the start of the regime of the present Left Front Government. While the first phase witnessed the passing of most of the tenancy acts, it was only under the rule of the Left Front Government that the main thrust was provided for their effective implementation.[2]

Keeping in mind the above background, the present chapter sets out three objectives: (a) to study the tenancy reform measures adopted in post-Independence Bengal; (b) to examine the changing structure of tenancy consequent upon the adoption of these measures; and (c) to note the major issues emanating from the recent phase of tenancy reforms in the state.

Tenancy Reform Measures in Post-Independence Bengal

Pre-1977 Measures

The first piece of tenancy legislation in West Bengal after Independence is the Bargadars Act of 1950. The Act stipulated that the bargadar and the landowner could choose any proportion acceptable to them for sharing the output. In case there was no such agreement, the bargadar would retain two-thirds of the gross output if

---

[2] For detailed discussion on the adoption and implementation of agrarian reform measures in post-Independence Bengal, one may refer to Dasgupta (1987).

he supplied all inputs of production. The bargadar could be evicted if the landowner required the land for self-cultivation or the bargadar misused/neglected the cultivation of such land. The Act empowered the government to set up 'conciliation boards' so as to settle the dispute, if any, between the bargadar and the landowner.

The West Bengal Estates Acquisition Act was passed in May 1953 (Ghosh and Dutt, 1977: 148–49). Its main objective was the abolition of intermediaries so as to bring all ryots and under-ryots into a direct relationship with the state. The Act, however, allowed the intermediaries to retain agricultural land in their *khas* possession up to 25 acres per capita. The Act also empowered the government to acquire the *khas* lands of any person if he did not cultivate it himself or got it cultivated by bargadars, provided the amount of such land exceeded 33 acres per owning individual.

Then came the West Bengal Land Reforms Act in 1955. It incorporated the provisions of the Bargadars Act (1950) with some changes. This Act underwent several amendments between 1955 and 1969. The main provisions of the Act in regard to the bargadars as amended up to 1969 are (*ibid.*: 149–51): (*a*) the landowner shall receive half of the gross produce if he supplied plough, cattle, manure and seed. In other cases, the proportion of output going to him shall be 40 per cent; (*b*) the place of threshing shall be decided mutually by the bargadar and the landowner; (*c*) if the produce of any land cultivated by a bargadar is harvested and taken away forcibly by a landowner, the bargadar shall be entitled to recover from such owner the share of the produce due to him or its money value; (*d*) the landowner shall be entitled to terminate a barga if the land cultivated by the bargadar plus the land under his personal cultivation does not exceed two-thirds of the total land (excluding homestead) owned by him.

In order to prevent concentration of land-ownership, the 1955 Act imposed a ceiling of 25 acres (excluding homestead) on the ownership holding of a ryot. As in other states, this provision, however, did not apply to lands comprising of orchards as well as lands held by religious and charitable institutions.

The passing of these Acts notwithstanding, the concentration of land-ownership could not be checked nor did the bargadars receive actual protection against eviction or their due share of the crop. As a matter of fact, the eviction of the bargadars started immediately after the passing of the 1950 Act (Government of India, 1976: 57).

Taking advantage of the loopholes of the 1955 Act, the landowners ejected a large number of bargadars. In fact, the highest number of bargadars were evicted during 1958–67 (Bandyopadhyay and Associates, 1983: 12–13; Bandyopadhyay, 1980: 26–28). The main defect in the Act was the provision of the landowner's right of resumption of land for personal cultivation if the land owned by him was within the limit set by the Act. This provision was fully exploited by the landowners and very often, the evicted bargadars were re-employed on the same land as agricultural labourers (Dasgupta, 1984c: A85). In the matter of implementation of ceiling laws too, not much success was achieved. The landowners and intermediaries displayed a great deal of ingenuity in dodging the effective implementation of the 1953 Act. Through redistribution within the family, mala fide transfers to relatives and friends and often to non-existent persons, a great deal of the ceiling surplus land was retained by the landowners (Bandyopadhyay and Associates, 1983: 14; Dasgupta, 1987: Ch. 1). Furthermore, full use was made of the legal exemptions given to the lands under orchards or religious and charitable institutions. All these tactics rendered the implementation of ceiling laws unsatisfactory.[3]

With the coming to power of the United Front Government by the close of the sixties, the agitation by the bargadars and the landless reached new heights leading to violent outbursts and forcible seizure of land from the jotedars. When the government collapsed in 1970, President's rule was imposed. At that time, the West Bengal Land Reforms Amendment Act was brought out (in 1970), possibly to check the continuing discontent among the bargadars and the landless. In 1970 (President's) Act, some important amendments were effected in the earlier 1955 Act with a

---

[3] It may be noted that at the time of the passing of the 1953 Act, it was hoped that about 37.3 per cent of arable land would be vested in the state. However, even by the 1980s only about 9.5 per cent was declared surplus. While till 1967 about 3.5 lakh acres of land was vested in the state, about 5 lakh acres were vested during the regime of United Front governments during 1967–70 alone when spontaneous seizure of ceiling surplus land by the sharecroppers and the landless became a mass phenomenon in West Bengal. See Dasgupta (1987: Ch.1); Ghosh (1981: A53). It is interesting to note that even with such a poor implementation of ceiling legislation, West Bengal ranked as the highest single contributor in the total pool of vested land in India at the end of the Sixth Five Year Plan. Out of the total vested land of 7.2 million acres in India, the share of West Bengal alone accounts for about 20 per cent while the state contains only 2.88 per cent of India's cultivated area. See Bandyopadhyay (1988: 24–25).

view to protecting the interest of the bargadars (Ghosh and Dutt, 1977: 151–52). These were: (*a*) the bargadar's right to cultivation was made hereditary; in case a bargadar died, the cultivation could be continued by his lawful heir; (*b*) the bargadar's share was raised to 75 per cent of gross produce if he supplied all the inputs and 50 per cent if all inputs except labour were supplied by the landowner; (*c*) the bargadar was entitled to a receipt from the landowner on delivery of his share of produce; (*d*) the place of threshing was to be decided by the bargadar; (*e*) no bargadar could be evicted as long as he continued to deliver his share of produce to the landowner; and (*f*) resumption of land for self-cultivation by the landowner was permissible only if lands so resumed together with other land under his personal cultivation did not exceed 3.0351 hectares; the resumption of land would also leave at least 0.8094 hectare with the bargadar.

In order to reduce the concentration of land-ownership, the West Bengal Land Reforms (Amendment) Act was passed in 1971. The main provisions were (*ibid.*: 152–54): (*a*) land owned by an adult unmarried person could not exceed 2.50 hectares in irrigated area or 3.50 hectares in unirrigated area; (*b*) land owned by a family consisting of five members could not exceed 5.0 standard (irrigated) hectares and 7.0 hectares in unirrigated lands. For a family consisting of more than five members, it was 5.0 standard hectares plus 0.5 standard hectares per each member in excess of five subject to a maximum limit of 7.0 standard hectares in irrigated lands or 9.80 hectares in unirrigated lands per family; and (*c*) the ceiling in the case of religious or charitable institutions was subject to the discretionary powers of the state government. As regards the bargadars, the Act stipulated that: (*a*) a bargadar cultivating land already vested in the state would be entitled to own up to 1 standard hectare of such land. The land cultivated by a bargadar is subject to a maximum limit of 6 hectares; and (*b*) surrender of land by the bargadar would not take effect unless verified and ascertained by the local official that the bargadar has left the cultivation voluntarily.

In addition to the above Acts, the government passed the West Bengal Acquisition of Homestead Land for Agricultural Labourers, Artisans and Fishermen Act in 1975. This Act transferred the ownership of homestead land to the landless agricultural labourers, sharecroppers and artisans up to a limit of 0.08 acre and the owners of such land were entitled to compensation from the government for the loss of their land.

What seems clear from the foregoing discussion is that several pieces of tenancy legislation were enacted in West Bengal prior to 1977 to protect the interests of the bargadars, many of which appeared fairly radical in nature. It is, however, a different story that not much attempt was made to put the legislation into effect.[4] What was more, the bargadars were denied their due share of the crop,[5] but many of them demanding protection under the law were in fact evicted and/or relegated to the status of agricultural labourers. Moreover, even a good part of ceiling surplus land captured by the bargadars and the landless during 1967–70 was taken back by the landowners during 1970–77 (Dasgupta, 1984c: A86).

Tenancy reforms since 1977

As mentioned earlier, the Left Front gained political power in West Bengal in 1977 mainly with the support of the peasants and agricultural labourers. The interest of these people has been accorded topmost priority in all its subsequent programmes. Interestingly, when the Left Front Government was formed in 1977,

[4] It may be noted that till about the mid-seventies, West Bengal shared the fate of other states as regards the non-implementation of land reform measures. Thus, the Draft Fifth Five Year Plan, while making an overall assessment of land reform programmes adopted in India since Independence candidly notes: 'the laws for the abolition of intermediary tenures have been implemented fairly efficiently whilst . . . tenancy reform and ceiling on holding legislation have fallen short of the desired objectives, and implementation of the enacted laws has been inadequate'. The Report of the Task Force on Agrarian Relations (1973) also writes: 'in no sphere of public activity in our country since Independence has the hiatus between percept and practice, between policy pronouncement and its actual execution been as great as the domain of land reform.' The Report pin-pointed 'lack of political will' as the key factor behind such ineffective implementation. For references see Government of India (1976: 46, 79); also see Bandyopadhyay (1988).

[5] A survey conducted in the early 1960s shows that the bargadars hardly obtained more than 50 per cent of gross output even when they carried all costs of production. Another survey conducted by Rudra in early 1970s in 81 villages spread over all districts of West Bengal shows the predominance of equal-sharing rule in West Bengal villages in the dominant crop season (aman paddy). The survey provides some evidence of sharing in the costs of some inputs such as seed, manure and fertilizer by the landowners, but in that case they received 50 per cent or more of gross output. See Government of India (1966: 142); Rudra (1975: A48).

there was not much legislative work left to be done in respect of tenancy reforms. It was essential, however, for the government to plug the loopholes in the existing legislation and strengthen its implementation. All the same, it has been a matter of controversy as to whether the government should have gone for more radical tenancy reform by abolishing landlordism and conferring the right of 'land to the tiller'. The policy of the government at this stage has, however, been speedy implementation of existing legislation because it perceives that:

> within the bounds of a constitution of a capitalist-landlord state, a constituent State Government cannot abolish the system of Zamindari, nor is it a feasible proposition. The State Government can only ameliorate the sufferings of the people to some extent, can rouse the village poor to mobilise and can enthuse them to strengthen their organising capacity. Through this process only, class enemy in the rural areas can be identified and cornered, thereby opening up new horizons for rural poor (Government of West Bengal, 1980: 1).

In keeping with its objective, the government amended the 1955 Act in September 1977 to protect the interest of the sharecroppers. Since, in the past, most of the sharecroppers had been evicted on the plea of resumption of land for 'personal cultivation' by the landowners, a new section was inserted into the amended Act of 1977 whereby the definition of 'personal cultivation' by the landowner was redefined. As it stands now, the landowner can resume his land given to a sharecropper if (Ghosh, 1986: 34–35): (a) he himself or some members of his family reside in the locality where land is situated; (b) income from land is the principal source of his income; (c) after the eviction of the bargadar, the land is cultivated by his own labour or by labour of a member of his family and not by hired labour; and (d) such resumption of land leaves a minimum of 2.5 acres with the sharecropper for continued cultivation. A further revision of the 1955 Act states that if anyone tries to evict any sharecropper illegally, he will be held responsible under the law and will be prosecuted accordingly. The landowners are also required to issue receipts failing which they are liable to pay a fine of Rs. 1,000 and/or to imprisonment for six months. The receipt which the sharecropper will receive will constitute the principal instrument for the recognition of his rights.

The most important in the Left Front Government's total package of programmes has been 'Operation Barga' (O.B.). O.B. has no new legislation but is a measure to record the names of the bargadars within the ambit of the 1955 Act. What is novel about O.B. is that the drive to register the names of the bargadars is undertaken with the collaboration of the groups of beneficiaries and with the active assistance of rural workers' organisations and self-governing institutions. Typically bureaucratic methods of recording the bargadars failed, in the past, to achieve any significant success. Individually, the bargadars have always been hesitant to come forward and register their names against the wishes of the landowners because of the fear of eviction. Hence in O.B., which was launched towards the end of 1978, the emphasis was 'to develop group action among potential beneficiaries to enable them to overcome the fear psychosis by creating a mutual support system' (Bandyopadhyay, 1980: 4). Moreover, in order to quicken the implementation of the programme, the following steps were generally followed (Ghosh, 1981: A51): (a) identification of priority areas with larger concentration of bargadars; (b) formation of official squads for continuously moving into these priority pockets; (c) conducting the meeting of the squad with the bargadars and the owners preferably in the evening and in a public place; (d) hearing both the parties by the government officials and examining documents, if any; and (e) passing the judgement and issuing the certificates to the bargadars whose names have been recorded.

The government also realized that merely registering the title of cultivation of the bargadars would not be very effective in improving their conditions unless meaningful steps were taken to break the ties of bondage this group might have had with the landlords and village money-lenders. The bargadars would generally depend on the jotedars for consumption loans, particularly during the lean season and the commercial banks would generally rate them ineligible for the receipt of bank loans, even for production purpose. Thus the government first made an experiment during the kharif season of 1978 with the help of five commercial banks and cooperatives to explore the possibilities of providing an alternative system of credit facility to the bargadars and assignees of vested land. The experiment was largely successful in spite of some initial administrative and operational difficulties. From 1979 onwards, the scheme has been vigorously implemented throughout the state in collaboration with eleven nationalized banks, seven gramin banks and the district central co-operative banks (Government of West Bengal, 1982: 7). For successful implementation of the programme, lists of the recorded bargadars and assignees of vested land, prepared and authenticated by designated revenue officials, are supplied to participating branches. Panchayats are then requested to sponsor cases while revenue and development staff are deployed to maintain documentation. In order to induce prompt repayment, the government introduced in 1979–80 full interest subsidy scheme for those who pay back the loan within the stipulated period. Moreover, revenue, panchayat and development agencies are instructed to join the campaign for prompt recovery of bank loans (Ghosh, 1981: A54).

It needs to be pointed out that the land reforms programme of the Left Front Government has been far more comprehensive and consists of more than the launching of O.B. scheme and of providing agricultural credit to the bargadars (Bandyopadhyay, 1980: 3–11; Dasgupta, 1987: Ch. 1). Soon after coming into power, the government endeavoured to detect and vest more ceiling surplus lands and distribute them among the landless and poor peasants. Consequently, while in the early seventies, West Bengal occupied the twelfth position among all Indian states in terms of declared land surplus, it was elevated to the first position only ten years later in 1981 (Lieten, 1990: 2265–66). Out of a total of 7.2 million acres of land vested with the government for all Indian states at the end of the Sixth Five-Year Plan, the share of West Bengal alone accounted for 20 per cent although its share in the total agricultural area of India stood at a meagre 3.2 per cent (Bandyopadhyay, 1986: A50, A55; Bandyopadhyay, 1988: 25).

The government also introduced the West Bengal Land Reforms (Amendment) Act 1981 (which was approved by the President of India in March 1986) with a view to plugging the loopholes in the earlier Acts relating to the ceiling of landholdings. This Act, along with its subsequent amendments (known as the West Bengal Land Reforms [Third Amendment] Act, 1986 and the West Bengal Land Reforms [Amendment] Act, 1990), sought to bring all classes of land under the ceiling provisions by withdrawing the exemptions earlier provided for religious/charitable trusts, plantations and fisheries. The recent amendments also provide for regulatory measures to check indiscriminate conversion of land from one use to another. It is, however, to be mentioned that the state is yet to achieve full implementation owing to orders of injunctions obtained by rural landed interests from the Calcutta High Court challenging the constitutional validity of the amendments.

Another priority area in the agrarian reform programmes of the Left Front Government has been promoting the interests of the class of agricultural labourers, many of whom are landless (see Dasgupta, 1984d: A143, A145). The programmes undertaken for them include: (a) distribution of ceiling surplus vested lands among the landless and the land-poor; (b) giving financial assistance in the form of subsidies to the assignees of vested land; (c) assigning permanent title for homestead purpose to all the landless agricultural workers up to 0.08 acre; and (d) creation of jobs through public works programme.

A noteworthy point regarding the agrarian reform programmes in West Bengal is that they are now implemented by the people's representatives in panchayats.[6] The panchayats are called upon to nominate the beneficiaries of vested land, monitor the implementation of public works activities in rural areas, promote the recording of bargadars along with performing many other functions. With the majority of the panchayat representatives belonging to the weaker sections, their direct involvement in planning and implementation of rural development programmes restructured the old power relations in the countryside and led to tremendous politicization of the poorer sections in West Bengal villages.

The programmes and policies of agrarian reform of the Left Front Government have been subjected to serious scrutiny by many researchers. However, as it is outside the purview of the present study to go into a full-length review of all its agrarian reform programmes, we take up for discussion in the last section of the present chapter the issues raised by scholars regarding the programmes relating to bargadars. Some of these issues will also be subjected to empirical verification in our subsequent chapters. For the moment, let us turn our attention towards examining the changing tenancy structure in the state since Independence.

Changing Tenancy Structure in West Bengal since Independence

We base our analysis of the changing structure of tenancy in West Bengal on the data thrown up by various rounds of the National

[6] For a detailed discussion of the panchayati raj system under the Left Front Government, see Datta, 1992.

Sample Survey (NSS). Actually, the NSS data are now available for four separate rounds, viz., the 8th Round (1953–54), the 16th Round (1960–61), the 26th Round (1971–72) and the 37th Round (1982). In so far as there is not much of a problem of comparability of data collected over various NSS rounds (Sanyal, 1988: 122–23), we could utilize data for all four points of time. However, we have dropped the 16th Round from our analysis because of non-availability of detailed information on many aspects of tenancy for that round. While delineating the changes in the tenancy structure in the state, our primary focus would be to see the changes between 1953–54 to 1971–72 (henceforth sub-period I) and 1971–72 to 1982 ('sub-period II). It may be recalled that most of the radical tenancy legislation was enacted in the beginning of the 1970s while most of their implementation is claimed to have been done since 1977 (see Dasgupta, 1987). That being so, sub-period II is likely to explain the changing pattern of tenancy consequent upon the implementation of tenancy reform measures.

Before we enter into the examination of tenancy structure proper, it would be worthwhile to start by looking at the changes in the pattern of landholding in the state. This is important because the distribution of landholdings not only determines the 'concentration of land' in the rural society but, to a great degree, also shapes the tenancy structure. Table 3.1 presents data on the distribution of ownership holdings at three points of time. In order to appreciate more fully as to how different landholding groups share the agricultural lands, we have divided them notionally into a few categories: (*a*) landless (less than 0.01 acre); (*b*) marginal (0.01–2.49 acres); (*c*) small (2.50–4.99 acres); (*d*) medium (5.00–9.99 acres); (*e*) big (10.00–14.99 acres); and (*f*) large (15.00 acres and above).

Table 3.1 admits of several important observations as regards the distribution of ownership holdings in the state: (*a*) About a fifth of the rural households were recorded as 'landless' in West Bengal in 1953–54. This declined significantly to less than a tenth in 1971–72. However, the figure for 1982 shows a fairly sharp rise in the percentage of the 'landless' (17.21 per cent). This is quite baffling considering the fact that West Bengal is considered one of the front-ranking states where land reform measures such as distribution of vested land to the landless proceeded at a fast rate,

Table 3.1
Distribution of Ownership Holdings in Rural West Bengal

Size Class (in acres)	Percentage of households			Percentage of owned area			Concentration ratio		
	1953–54	1971–72	1982	1953–54	1971–72	1982	1953–54	1971–72	1982
Less than 0.01 (Landless)	20.54	9.78	17.21	–	–	–	–	–	–
0.01–2.49 (Marginal)	52.92	67.83	64.38	15.90	27.27	30.33	0.30	0.40	0.47
2.50–4.99 (Small)	12.61	12.65	11.50	18.60	25.69	28.77	1.48	2.03	2.50
5.00–9.99 (Medium)	8.56	7.30	5.54	25.51	27.72	27.23	2.98	3.78	4.92
10.00–14.99 (Big)	2.76	1.72	1.09	13.99	11.55	9.47	5.07	6.72	8.69
15.00 & above (Large)	2.60	0.72	0.28	26.00	7.77	4.20	10.00	10.79	15.00
All sizes	100.00	100.00	100.00	100.00	100.00	100.00	–	–	–

Sources: (a) N.S.S. Report No. 66; 8th Round (1953–54).
(b) N.S.S. Report No. 215.21; 26th Round (1971–72).
(c) N.S.S. Report No. 330; 37th Round (1982).

Notes: Concentration ratio is defined as the ratio of percentage of area owned to percentage of households.
Average size of holding (in acres): 1953–54 = 2.39; 1971–72 = 1.73; 1982 = 1.36.
Gini Ratio: 1953–54 = 0.73; 1971–72 = 0.67; 1982 = 0.70.

particularly, in recent years.[7] (*b*) Although the proportion of households in the 'marginal' category increased during sub-period I, a decline in the same is noticeable in sub-period II. However, if households in the 'landless' and 'marginal' categories are put together, a continuous increase in the percentage of households under these categories is observed in West Bengal. These two categories together constituted nearly 73 per cent, 77 per cent and 82 per cent of all households respectively in 1953–54, 1971–72 and 1982. (*c*) There took place a decline in the percentage of 'small' households during sub-period II. The decline in the percentage of households in 'marginal' and 'small' categories is, however, associated with an increase in the percentage of area owned by them. As a result, there took place an increase in the 'concentration ratio'[8] for these categories. In other words, in spite of a decline in terms of the percentage of households, these categories consolidated their position in respect of owned area in 1982 compared with 1971–72. (*d*) The decline in the percentage of households is also noticeable in the 'middle', 'big' and 'large' categories. However, in their case, the rate of decline of the percentage of owned area has been lower than the rate of decline in the percentage of households. This resulted in an increase in their concentration ratios over time. It may also be noted that while in 1953–54, the 'middle' categories of owners comprised 8.56 per cent of rural households and occupied 25.51 per cent of owned area, in 1982, the corresponding figures were 5.54 per cent and 27.23 per cent respectively. The increase in the percentage of owned area despite the fall in the percentage of households in the 'middle' category clearly indicates increased concentration of land with them in West Bengal in recent years. (*e*) Another important point to note is that the 'big' and 'large' categories together comprised 1.37 per cent of households but they accounted for 13.67 per cent of owned area in 1982.

All the above observations lead us to the conclusion that although the 'marginal' and 'small' owners consolidated their positions to some extent in terms of area owned, it is the 'middle' categories of

---

[7] It may be noted that the decline in 'landlessness' has been an all-India phenomenon between 1952–53 and 1971–72. However, between 1971–72 and 1982, the proportion of 'landless' increased in most of the states as well as for India as a whole. See Sanyal (1988: 127); Haque (1987: 318).

[8] Concentration ratio is defined as the ratio of percentage of area owned to percentage of households.

owners who have benefited the most in terms of area-shift in the recent years. Nevertheless, quite a substantial proportion of area in West Bengal is still occupied by the 'big' and 'large' categories of owners. These developments along with the increase in landlessness explain the high degree of inequality in the distribution of ownership holdings as late as 1982. In fact, for West Bengal, there took place a small increase in the inequality of distribution of ownership holdings in 1982 compared with 1971–72. This is revealed by the value of Gini Ratios of 0.67 in 1970–71 and 0.70 in 1982.[9]

We now come to the study of the changing pattern of operational holdings in the state. Operational holdings by taking cognizance of land-leasing by the households, provide a better idea of their relative economic position. As before, we examine the distribution of operational holdings by dividing the households into several categories.

Table 3.2 brings out a few important features: First, the largest section of the rural households in West Bengal belonged to the category of 'marginal' farmers and the extent of 'marginalization' increased over time. While 64.51 per cent of operational holdings belonged to this category in 1953–54, they increased to 74.32 per cent in 1982. Second, although the percentage of holdings in 'small' and 'medium' categories increased in sub-period I, a clear decline is noticeable in sub-period II. For other categories, percentage of holdings declined consistently over the years. For all these categories, except the 'small', percentage of operated area declined. However, as the percentage of operated area declined at a rate lower than the percentage of holdings, there took place increase in their concentration ratios. Third, the distribution of operational holdings is also far from being equal. Even in 1982, while about 90 per cent of holdings at the bottom (marginal and small categories) operated about 58 per cent of area, only 1.77 per cent of holdings at the top ('big' and 'large' categories) accounted for 13.71 per cent of area operated. Moreover, 8.07 per cent of households in the middle range control 28.25 per cent of operated area in West Bengal today. Fourth, the average size of operational holding in the state has declined gradually, particularly in sub-period II. In 1982, the average size of operational holding for the state stood at 1.91 acres only.

---

[9] In order to calculate the Gini Ratio, we have used data given for all possible size classes in the NSS reports.

Table 3.2

Distribution of Operational Holdings in Rural West Bengal

Size Class (in acres)	Percentage of households			Percentage of operated area			Concentration ratio		
	1953–54	1971–72	1982	1953–54	1971–72	1982	1953–54	1971–72	1982
Less than 2.50 (Marginal)	64.51	61.20	74.32	14.29	24.81	29.27	0.22	0.41	0.39
2.50–4.99 (Small)	17.74	22.80	15.83	23.01	28.91	28.77	1.30	1.27	1.82
5.00–9.99 (Medium)	12.48	12.94	8.07	31.32	31.06	28.25	2.51	2.40	3.50
10.00–14.99 (Big)	2.91	2.12	1.36	12.42	8.78	8.51	4.27	4.14	6.26
15.00 & above (Large)	2.36	0.94	0.41	18.96	6.44	5.20	8.03	6.85	12.68
All sizes	100.00	100.00	100.00	100.00	100.00	100.00	–	–	–

Sources: (a) N.S.S. Report No. 66; 8th Round (1953–54).
(b) N.S.S. Report No. 215.21; 26th Round (1971–72).
(c) N.S.S. Report No. 331; 37th Round (1982).

Notes: Concentration ratio is defined as the ratio of percentage of area operated to percentage of holdings.
Average size of holding (in acres): 1953–54 = 2.77; 1971–72 = 2.76; 1982 = 1.91.
Gini Ratio: 1953–54 = 0.65; 1971–72 = 0.65; 1982 = 0.60.

Having outlined the changes in the distribution of ownership and operational holdings, we now turn towards examination of the changes in the tenancy structure in the state since Independence. In this regard, our main point of inquiry would be to find out the changes in the pattern of land-leasing, composition of lessors and lessees and the types of tenancy in the state.

Table 3.3 presents information on the leasing out operation by various ownership categories in the state. The first point to note is that for all categories of owners, there took place a continuous decline between 1953–54 and 1982, both in the percentage of households as well as the percentage of owned area leased out. Thus, while 10.41 per cent of all owners leased out their land in 1953–54, and 9.48 per cent in 1971–72, the figure in 1982 is sharply reduced to a mere 3.71 per cent. Although this may be due in part to under-reporting by the lessors, a large part of this decline may be attributed to landowners' fear of the enforcement of tenancy laws on their leased out land, particularly, in recent years. Secondly, the incidence of the leasing out of land has not been the same for all categories of owners. The higher categories generally tended to reveal a higher propensity to lease out their land. Accordingly, the percentage of households leasing out as well as the percentage of owned area leased out have been greater for the higher categories of owners. Third, although the practice of leasing out is found to be greater for the higher categories of owners, the percentage of households leasing out has not been insignificant for 'small' and 'medium' categories either. In 1982, 8.74 per cent of 'small' and 13.84 per cent of 'medium' owners leased out their land. Fourth, the fact that the higher categories of owners reflect a greater tendency to lease out their land does not necessarily mean that the majority of the lessors would come from them. This is particularly the case where 'marginal' and 'small' owners dominate the rural scene. Thus when we consider the distribution of households leasing out into various categories (Table 3.4), it is found that the majority of lessors in West Bengal actually come from the lower categories. Not only that the share of 'marginal' holdings in the distribution of all households leasing out has been the highest at each point of time, but their share actually increased over the years. Another point to note in this context is that the shares of 'medium', 'big' and 'large' categories in the distribution of households leasing out declined in 1982 compared with 1953–54 and those of 'marginal'

Table 3.3
Leasing-out Operation by Ownership Size Groups in Rural West Bengal

Size Class (in acres)	Percentage of households leasing out			Percentage of owned area leased out			Area leased out per household leasing out (in acres)		
	1953–54	1971–72	1982	1953–54	1971–72	1982	1953–54	1971–72	1982
0.01–2.49 (Marginal)	8.26	7.34	2.52	9.96	7.91	1.75	0.87	0.78	0.47
2.50–4.99 (Small)	14.66	14.34	8.74	10.09	9.59	3.17	2.43	2.34	1.23
5.00–9.99 (Medium)	22.68	12.90	13.84	12.07	7.89	2.18	3.80	4.00	1.05
10.00–14.99 (Big)	33.90	31.97	24.26	17.61	11.22	2.47	6.30	4.07	1.20
10.00 & above (Large)	50.45	38.38	18.54	25.04	11.09	4.99	11.90	5.41	5.37
All classes	10.41	9.48	3.71	15.51	8.95	2.48	3.57	1.80	0.91

Source: As in Table 3.1.

Table 3.4

*Distribution of Households Leasing-out and Leasing-in
in Rural West Bengal (Percentage)*

Size Class (in acres)	1953–54		1971–72		1982	
	HLO	HLI	HLO	HLI	HLO	HLI
0.01–2.49 (Marginal)	42.03	62.35	55.36	57.68	62.35	73.05
2.50–4.99 (Small)	17.75	19.81	22.62	29.72	19.81	16.75
5.00–9.99 (Medium)	18.65	14.37	11.74	11.24	14.37	9.07
10.00–14.99 (Big)	8.99	2.20	6.85	1.10	2.20	0.94
15.00 & above (Large)	12.58	1.27	3.43	0.26	1.27	0.19
Total	100.00	100.00	100.00	100.00	100.00	100.00

Sources: (a) N.S.S. Report No. 66; 8th Round (1953–54).
　　　　 (b) N.S.S. Report No. 215.21; 26th Round (1971–72).
　　　　 (c) N.S.S. Report Nos. 330 and 331; 37th Round (1982).
Notes: HLO = Households leasing out; HLI = Households leasing in.

and 'small' categories increased. While 47.76 per cent of all households leasing out belonged to 'marginal' and 'small' categories in 1953–54, the corresponding figure becomes 82.16 per cent in 1982.

Data on leasing-in operation are presented in Table 3.5. Several points emerge from the table: (a) As in the case of leasing out, there took place a continuous decline in the percentage of holdings reporting area leased in as well as the percentage of operated area leased in by all categories of operators in the state. For the state as a whole, while 41.49 per cent of holdings reported area leased-in in 1953–54, the corresponding figure for 1982 got reduced to 22.15 per cent. Moreover, the percentage of operated area leased in declined from 25.45 per cent in 1953–54 to 12.34 per cent in 1982. This clearly indicates that tenancy cultivation has been on the decline in West Bengal, as in most other states.[10] The declining tendency towards tenant cultivation could be due to several factors

---

[10] The fact that tenancy is declining in West Bengal has also been reported by Bardhan and Rudra (1978: 381) from their survey of 110 villages in 1975–76. Also see Swamy (1988).

Table 3.5
Leasing-in Operation by Size Groups of Operational Holdings in Rural West Bengal

Size Class (in acres)	Percentage of holdings reporting area leased in			Percentage of operated area leased in			Area leased-in per holding leasing in (acres)		
	1953-54	1971-72	1982	1953-54	1971-72	1982	1953-54	1971-72	1982
0.01-2.49 (Marginal)	40.09	32.57	22.58	28.92	25.82	13.25	0.44	0.88	0.44
2.50-4.99 (Small)	46.34	45.06	24.04	32.94	24.08	11.27	2.41	1.87	1.62
5.00-9.99 (Medium)	47.78	30.04	25.56	31.63	14.51	11.12	4.60	3.20	2.90
10.00-14.99 (Big)	31.40	17.90	15.34	17.83	5.68	4.54	6.71	3.64	3.52
15.00 & above (Large)	22.45	9.50	12.11	8.43	6.85	5.31	8.37	13.72	8.46
All classes	41.49	34.15	22.15	25.45	18.73	12.34	1.70	1.50	1.03

Source: As in Table 3.2.

Note: The N.S.S. report for 1982 shows 27 pure-tenant holdings operating 50.00 acres and above which we have not included in our analysis.

such as sub-division of land through inheritances, eviction of tenants following tenancy legislation, redistribution of ceiling-surplus land among hitherto sharecroppers and landless, reluctance on the part of the landowners to initiate fresh tenancy arrangements for fear of tenancy legislation awarding the sharecropper a higher proportion of crop and shielding him against eviction and so on (Sengupta, 1981: A89). An important reason towards decline in tenancy in recent years could also be the spread of new technology in agriculture which made cultivation with hired labour more attractive to many landowners (Dasgupta, 1984c: A93).

The second important point to note from Table 3.5 is that the practice of leasing in is relatively higher in the lower categories. Among them, however, 'marginal', 'small' and 'medium' categories have responded almost equally in the matter of leasing in land in West Bengal. Thus, in 1982, while 22.58 per cent of 'marginal' operators reported area leased in, the corresponding figures for 'small' and 'medium' categories have been 24.04 per cent and 25.56 per cent respectively. The proportion of households reporting area leased in have not been insignificant for the 'big' and 'large' categories also. Although the percentage of households reporting area leased in declined significantly in lower categories, particularly, during sub-period II, such decline is not very prominent for 'big' and 'large' categories. This means that some households in the higher categories too involve themselves in leasing in land signifying the presence of 'reverse tenancy', though not as intensively as in some green revolution areas of India.[11]

Third, if we consider the distribution of holdings leasing in into various categories (Table 3.4 above), it is observed that a majority of such holdings fall in the 'marginal' category. The share of this category in total holdings reporting area leased in increased further over the years (from 62.35 per cent in 1953–54 to 73.05 per cent in 1982). Next to follow are the 'small' and 'medium' groups (16.75 per cent and 9.07 per cent respectively in 1982). In as much as the majority of households leasing out land as well as the holdings leasing in come from 'marginal', 'small' and 'medium' categories (this is more prominent in 1982), any radical policy towards tenancy

[11] For some recent evidence in green revolution areas, one may refer to Singh (1989: A86–A92).

reform is likely to affect these categories of households most in West Bengal.

An important aspect of the change in tenancy structure in West Bengal since Independence is the decline in the importance of entirely leased in holdings. As shown in Table 3.6, the entirely leased in holdings in the state declined from 21.20 per cent of operational holdings in 1953–54 to 7.52 per cent in 1982. This may be due to the eviction of large number of poor tenants who are pushed to the rank of agricultural labourers. This may also explain in part the increase in the percentage of agricultural labourers in West Bengal since Independence.[12] Partly leased in holdings represented much higher percentage in total operational holdings in 1982 (15.83 per cent) compared with entirely leased in holdings.[13] Another important point to note is that the percentage of entirely leased in holdings is higher in the lower size classes.

As regards the types of tenancy, Table 3.7 clearly demonstrates the importance of share tenancy as the dominant form of tenancy in the state. In 1971–72, 92.58 per cent of total leased in area was under share tenancy. Although, over the years, there took place a big decline in the importance of share tenancy, about 56 per cent of leased in area could still be found to be under share tenancy in 1982. This decline is associated with an increase in the percentage of leased in area under fixed rent tenancy (increasing from 3.42 per cent in 1971–72 to 14.75 per cent in 1982). In other words, there is a clear shift away from share-tenancy to fixed-rent tenancy in West Bengal. Another interesting point to note is that while the lower categories of holdings prefer to lease in land more on share tenancy, the higher categories tend to represent a higher percentage of leased in area under fixed-rent tenancy. This trend is more clearly observed in 1982. This is understandable for, with the penetration of new technology in agriculture, higher categories of

---

[12] It may be noted that the percentage of agricultural labourers in total rural workforce increased in West Bengal from 18.97 per cent in 1951 to 32.95 per cent in 1981. See Dasgupta (1984*d*: A141).

[13] This is at variance with the general presumption in most of the neoclassical models on tenancy that the tenants are completely landless. The fact that the land-lease market is actually dominated by 'mixed' categories (i.e., owner-cum-tenants), rather than by 'pure' tenants is also emphasized by Dantwala and Shah (1971: 194) in their study of some regions in Maharashtra and Gujarat.

Table 3.6

Percentages of Entirely Owned, Entirely Leased-in and Mixed Holdings by Size Groups of Operational Holdings in Rural West Bengal

Size Class (in acres)	Entirely owned			Entirely leased-in			Partly leased-in		
	1953–54	1971–72	1982	1953–54	1971–72	1982	1953–54	1971–72	1982
0.01–2.49 (Marginal)	59.91	67.43	76.72	28.65	3.79	9.06	11.44	28.78	14.22
2.50–4.99 (Small)	53.66	54.94	71.55	10.84	2.55	0.66	35.50	42.51	20.62
5.00–9.99 (Medium)	52.22	69.97	74.92	5.78	2.91	4.83	42.00	27.12	20.25
10.00–14.99 (Big)	68.60	82.10	87.41	1.65	–	–	29.75	17.90	12.59
15.00 & above (Large)	77.75	90.50	89.24	1.02	–	–	21.33	9.50	10.76
All classes	58.51	65.44	76.65	21.20	3.28	7.52	20.29	31.28	15.83

Sources: As in Table 3.2.

Table 3.7
Leased-in Area by Types of Tenancy in Rural West Bengal

Size Class (in acres)	Percentage of operated area under				Percentage of leased-in area under			
	Share tenancy		Fixed-rent tenancy		Share tenancy		Fixed-rent tenancy	
	1971–72	1982	1971–72	1982	1971–72	1982	1971–72	1982
0.01–2.49 (Marginal)	23.41	9.38	0.81	1.33	90.70	70.71	3.14	9.25
2.50–4.99 (Small)	22.64	8.94	1.06	1.19	94.02	79.33	4.40	10.56
5.00–9.99 (Medium)	13.78	6.50	0.42	3.60	94.93	58.39	2.91	32.33
10.00–14.99 (Big)	10.19	1.85	–	0.92	100.00	40.86	–	20.20
15.00 & above (Large)	4.48	–	–	0.77	65.61	–	–	14.48
All classes	17.34	6.85	0.64	1.82	92.58	55.83	3.42	14.75

Sources: (a) N.S.S. Report No. 215.21; 26th Round (1971–72).
(b) N.S.S. Report No. 331; 37th Round (1982).

lessees are not possibly willing to share the benefits of improved cultivation with the lessors.[14]

We may now summarize the broad pattern of changes in land-holding and tenancy structure in the state since Independence. The analysis of distribution of ownership holdings in West Bengal reveals that the incidence of landlessness has increased over time. The percentage of the landless and marginal owners together showed a rising tendency. For all other categories, there took place a decline in the percentage of households. However, a decline in the percentage of households in the case of middle category of owners (owning 5.00–9.99 acres) is accompanied by an increase in the percentage of owned area. This implies increased concentration of lands in the hands of the owners in this category. Quite a substantial proportion of area is still owned by 'big' and 'large' owners in West Bengal. This along with the rise in the percentage of the 'landless' explains the increase in inequality of ownership holdings in the state.

The study of operational holdings indicates the increase in the percentage of 'marginal' holdings over time. Nearly three-fourths of the operational holdings fell in this category in 1982. The distribution of operational holdings is also far from being equal. The average size of operational holding declined continuously in West Bengal and it stood at 1.91 acres in 1982.

There has been a general tendency towards a decline in the practice of leasing out land by all categories of owners. This is particularly true in the years since 1971–72. Although the percentage of households leasing out seems to be greater for higher categories of owners, the percentage of households leasing out in 'small' and 'medium' categories has not been insignificant even in 1982. If we consider the distribution of all households leasing out into various ownership groups, it is found that majority of the lessors in West Bengal belong to the 'marginal' and 'small' categories of owners. Furthermore, the percentage share of these two categories in all households leasing out increased in 1982 compared with the preceding periods.

[14] Ghosh (1981: 158) in his study of two villages in Burdwan district of West Bengal observes how the lease market for land underwent several changes with the coming of new technology. He notes, *inter alia*, that sharecropping is more prevalent among the small farmers compared to large farmers who now prefer fixed rent tenancy.

A general decline in the practice of leasing in land is also noticeable in West Bengal for all categories of operators. In 1982, 12.84 per cent of operated area in the state was under tenant cultivation. The decline in tenanted area is also accompanied by a decline in the percentage of the entirely leased in holdings. This means that many of the erstwhile pure tenants have been evicted and possibly pushed into the army of agricultural labourers.

Although the percentage of holdings reporting area leased in as well as the percentage of operated area leased in have been higher for the lower categories, quite a substantial percentage of holdings in higher categories reported area leased in. This gives some evidence about the presence of 'reverse tenancy' in West Bengal, though not as intensively as is reported in some green revolution areas of India. The distribution of leasing in holdings shows that a vast majority of such holdings belong to the 'marginal' category and the shares of 'small' and 'medium' categories come next in order. In so far as the majority of households leasing out as well as leasing in belong to these lower categories, it is perhaps fair to say that the practice of land-leasing in West Bengal has been a phenomenon largely confined to marginal, and to some extent, small and medium categories of households.

Share tenancy has been the dominant form of tenancy in the state although a clear decline in its importance is discernible in recent years. There has been a tendency, in recent years, towards a shift away from share tenancy to fixed-rent tenancy. However, its total impact has so far made only a marginal difference on the overall tenancy structure of the state and share tenancy continues to predominate as the principal form of tenancy. The percentage of leased-in area under share tenancy has been generally higher for lower categories while that under fixed rent tenancy has been greater in higher categories of holdings. This possibly reflects the reluctance of bigger lessees in recent years not to share through crop-sharing arrangements the benefits of improved cultivation under changing agricultural conditions.

Recent Phase of Tenancy Reforms: Some Issues

In this section, we take stock of the major issues being debated by various scholars as regards the recent phase of tenancy reforms in

West Bengal, particularly in respect of the programme of O.B. It may be recalled that the purpose of O.B. has been to record all bargadars within a certain period so as to provide security to their tenure and entitle them to the stipulated share of produce as also to credit facilities from institutional agencies for production purpose. In consonance with these objectives, some modifications to the tenancy legislation have also been made. However, the programme of O.B. has been subjected to serious criticism by many scholars. While many of the criticisms question the justification of such a programme from an economic point of view, others raise doubt against the whole strategy of agrarian transformation being pursued recently in West Bengal of which O.B. is an important part.

The most formidable criticisms against O.B. have been voiced by Rudra (1981: A65) and Khasnabis (1981, 1982). On the economic front, Rudra argues that (a) barga recording has not led to any gain in the income of the bargadars; (b) the bargadars who have recorded their names have not been able to use much of modern inputs than before; (c) recording of names by the bargadars has choked the flow of production advances from the landlords to the bargadars; and (d) sharing of cost by the landowners which was gradually emerging as a normal phenomenon in West Bengal has been replaced by non-participation in cost by them. Rudra's other objections are perhaps more interesting. He argues that: (1) barga recording has actually failed to weaken the grip of the rich farmers in as much as nearly 50 per cent of the bargadars have not recorded their names; (2) O.B. does not aim at abolition but the perpetuation of tenancy; and (3) the barga system is by no means the foundation of West Bengal's agriculture and the bargadars are by no means the most important section of the toiling masses. In his view, agricultural labourers constitute the most exploited and oppressed section of the rural population but their interest has been sacrificed under the Left Front rule.

Khasnabis praises the genuine political will of the government to promote the interests of the bargadars. But, in a vein similar to that of Rudra, he explains how the semi-feudal authority of land-lords exercises their control over the tenants to frustrate even a 'reformist' policy such as O.B. In his view, 'O.B. which tries to record the rights of tenants approved the intermediary rights of the landowners too. Thus the rent earning authority of non-cultivators, condemned by the bourgeoise democratic revolution, gets a communist sanction. This is the fundamental weakness of the policies adopted by the Left Front Government for the promotion of the interests of the bargadars' (Khasnabis, 1981: A44).

There are other criticisms too against O.B. Dutt (1981) is doubtful how long the bargadars can sustain their strength in the absence of economic viability. Bereft of institutional finance and marketing facilities, he argues, the bargadars are bound to the landowner-cum-usurer. He further argues that the Left Front Government seems to have underestimated the degree of penetration of usury and merchant capital in the rural economy. If this were appreciated, more efforts should have been made to consolidate landholdings of poor peasants, to unite them through various forms of cooperatives which would include labourers but definitely exclude landowners who exploit other's labour. He concludes: 'What seems to be missing still is a sense of direction of the agrarian programme in its broad framework' (Dutt, 1981: A60). Sengupta (1981: A72) goes on to argue that with near completion of the land reform programmes of the first phase (the so-called democratic phase) in West Bengal in terms of abolition of intermediary interests, acquiring of surplus land for redistribution and barga tenancy reform, the agrarian policies of the Left government have reached their 'saturation point'. He, therefore, asks: 'where does one go from here?'

Having noted the main objections against the programme of O.B., it may be in order to offer brief comments on some of them here. First, regarding Rudra's objections, it would perhaps be fair to say that whether the recorded bargadars suffered loss of income or failed to use modern inputs is essentially an empirical question and can be answered only through a careful scrutiny of empirical data at the grass-roots level. In this connection, whatever evidence is available so far does show some cases where the bargadars have gained in terms of higher yield after recording (see Dasgupta, 1987: Ch. II; Lieten, 1990: 2269–70). This could be due to two reasons: (*a*) recording by providing security of their tenure motivates them to exert greater effort on barga land; and (*b*) bargadars do also avail of other facilities, such as institutional finance, after recording. Nevertheless, we do admit that detailed empirical studies need to be undertaken for seeking definitive judgement on this aspect. As regards the landowners' participation in costs prior to barga recording, there is no clear evidence to suggest that such participation has been total (that is, the landowners shared in all cost of production other than labour). The available evidence indicates that landowners generally participate in one item of cost or the other (mostly fertilizers and/or irrigation) and this results in bargadars sacrificing the share of the crop as stipulated in the tenancy legislation. This can also be corroborated by the studies conducted by Rudra himself. He reported that landowners participated fully or partly in costs of seed, manures and fertilizer only when they obtained 50 per cent or more of gross output (see Rudra, 1975b; Bardhan and Rudra, 1980: 289). In other words, sharing of costs by the landowners prior to recording did not necessarily ensure that the tenants received their due share of the crop: cost-sharing was actually motivated by the landowners to extract from the tenants a share of the crop larger than that stipulated in the tenancy legislation.

The observation that a large section of tenants has not responded to O.B. seems to have been made on the presumption that there are about 2 million bargadars in West Bengal of whom only about half were recorded till the end of 1980. In fact, the exact number of bargadars in the state has long been a matter of wide guess. Even in the official circles, it has been believed that the total number of bargadars would be between 2 and 2.5 million (see Government of West Bengal; 1980: i–ii). However, a recent estimate places the figure at 1.5 million (see Bandyopadhyay and Associates, 1983: 30). In any case, the available information on the number of bargadars recorded shows that the performance of the programme has been quite satisfactory. Thus, while up to early 1979 about 0.52 million bargadars had recorded their names, the number of recorded bargadars increased gradually to more than 1.44 million by the end of 1992.[15] Nevertheless, it is possible that there are still some rural pockets with a relatively higher concentration of the unrecorded bargadars. It is as possible that the recent estimate of 1.5 million bargadars is on the lower side. The aforementioned facts are, however, not adequate to prove that barga recording has not met with success.

[15] The data on the number of bargadars recorded are obtained from the Directorate of Land Records and Survey, Government of West Bengal.

The other question of abolishing landlordism and providing 'land to the tiller' too requires serious attention indeed. In this context, Bose (1981: 2059) argues that under the present set-up where an individual state government is subject to the political and constitutional limitations imposed on it, it is not possible to contemplate the complete abolition of tenancy without nationalization of land. Dasgupta (1984c: A89) goes further to clarify the short-term and long-term objectives of the Left Front in West Bengal. The long-term objective is surely to capture state power at the national level through democratic revolution. The leadership of this revolution would be firmly in the hands of the working class and its ally, the peasantry. Its main objective would be to abolish landlordism and place the land in the hands of those who actually till the land. However, such an objective cannot be immediately translated into a realizable programme unless the state power in the country as a whole were to be captured by the working class by replacing the 'bourgeois-democratic regime'. Dasgupta further argues that it would be wrong to compare this long-term objective with the short-term objective at the state level because what can be attained by an individual state within the confines of the 'bourgeois-landlord Constitution' cannot be equated with what can be attained at the national level in the long term after the transfer of power to the working class and peasantry.

Rudra's assertion that the bargadars' interest has been over-emphasized and that of agricultural labourers sacrificed under the Left Front regime cannot be accepted as such. If one peeps into the history of the sharecropping system in Bengal, it would clearly emerge that the sharecroppers have been subjected to all sorts of exploitation under the colonial rule and for many years even after Independence. Under this situation, there can possibly be no better alternative than safeguarding their interest, through a programme such as O.B., within the confines of the Constitution which recognises private property rights. It is also wrong to place the interest of sharecroppers in contradiction with the interest of agricultural labourers because, in actuality, many of the sharecroppers would also act as agricultural labourers. Furthermore, whether or not one accepts Rudra's method of differentiation of agrarian classes, there can possibly be little doubt regarding his own identification of the 'exploited' class in rural areas comprising agricultural labourers classified in official statistics as well as the small and marginal farmers many of whom might also be tenants (see Rudra, 1982: 440). This being so, O.B. clearly serves the interest of the 'exploited' class in rural areas. Actually Rudra's comments on the subject create the impression that there has not been any programme for agricultural labourers. This is not quite true. As we have mentioned earlier, various programmes have recently been taken up to improve the conditions of agricultural labourers in West Bengal. It is, however, outside the purview of the present study to attempt an in-depth analysis of the adequacy of such programmes. Confining ourselves to the objectives of our study, we shall rather focus our analysis on tenancy issues and, accordingly, the sharecroppers are the main concern of our inquiry in the subsequent chapters.

4

Participants in the Land-Lease Market: Options and Constraints

In the literature on the structure of the land-lease market, two contrasting views are generally put forward. One view projects the tenant as the weaker party and the terms and conditions of lease are then purported to be dictated by the stronger party, namely, the landlord. Thus, the market for land-lease is seen as a source of exploitation of the tenant. This is reinforced where the land-lease market is interlocked with other markets such as credit, commodity and/or labour (Bharadwaj, 1974: 5; Bell and Srinivasan, 1989; Reddy, 1992). Some proponents of this view also project tenancy as a semi-feudal institution which inhibits agricultural modernization (see Bhaduri, 1973; Prasad, 1974). At the other extreme, it has been argued that the tenants do not necessarily constitute the weaker party; rather, the 'exploiter-exploited' relationship gets transformed into one where the better-off landed farmers lease in land to augment their farm size further from the owners of petty holdings for whom self-cultivation turns out to be uneconomical. This is claimed to happen more particularly with the penetration of new technology in agriculture.[1] It has been added further that 'tenancy arrangement as such has nothing feudal about it; it is perfectly compatible with capitalist relations between owners of land and tenants of land' (Rudra, 1982: 128–29).

Whether or not the tenants form a weaker party and tenancy represents a semi-feudal institution is subject to empirical judgement. There is indeed scope for detailed empirical work explaining the intricacies of the land-lease market and its dynamics. Before

[1] See in particular, Vyas (1970: A75); Rao (1974: A58); Bharadwaj and Das (1975: 239); Bardhan (1976: 1544); Nadkarni (1976: A137–A139); Singh (1989: A88).

we enter into a discussion on the subject, with the help of fresh field data gathered from West Bengal agriculture, we would like to emphasize here that the lease market for land can actually take on a different character at different stages in history. Thus, at one stage, it may represent a situation where the tenants do indeed comprise the weaker party and are subjected to all kinds of exploitation by their landlords.[2] This may also prove detrimental to the progress of agriculture. A departure from this weak-strong brand of agrarian relationship may be contemplated in the course of historical development, whereby the tenants acquire considerable power, political and otherwise, through their organized struggle against exploitation by feudal landlords. This means that under the changed circumstances, with tenants enjoying some degree of collective and organized strength, often backed by political parties, tenancy relations are likely to appear as a different proposition than the one that might have prevailed under the old situation. This is an aspect which, unfortunately, has not received adequate attention, presumably because of the excessive preoccupation of past researchers with the impact of changing technology on the tenancy structure, often confined to a given historical phase of tenancy relations.[3] In the specific context of West Bengal, however, the issue of the possible restructuring of tenancy relations in the face of an almost continuous chain of tenant struggles, particularly in the aftermath of the organized struggle in the recent past, becomes as important as the other issue of impact of technical change on tenancy structure.

To reiterate, there has been an organized mobilization of tenants along with other poorer sections in rural Bengal by the Left parties, more vigorously since the late sixties, which led to the formation of Left Coalition Government firstly for two brief periods between 1969 and 1970 and then the Left Front Government continuously from 1977 onwards. On assuming power in 1977, the Left Front Government launched, *inter alia*, the programme of Operation Barga (O.B.) The basic purpose of this programme was to organize and mobilize the tenants in their struggle against rural vested interests. Under this programme, an organized campaign

[2] For example, the conditions prevailing in pre-Independence Bengal are very largely akin to such a situation.

[3] Most of the recent studies on tenancy ignore the issue of changing tenancy situation following organized movements by the tenants.

was undertaken to record the names of bargadars (sharecroppers) and they were given legal protection against rent enhancement and illegal eviction by the landlords. These recorded tenants were also to be provided with institutional credit in order to free them from the clutches of usurer-landlords and rural money-lenders. Quite naturally, such effective intervention by the Left Front Government has been responsible for authenticating the tenancy rights of a very large section of bargadars in rural Bengal. This, however, does not necessarily imply that all the tenants in West Bengal have recorded their names through programmes such as O.B. In fact, in some pockets, there are still some tenants who have not chosen to get themselves recorded as tenants. Consequently, such tenants are involved in what may be termed as the traditional form of tenancy arrangements.[4] Thus, one way of explaining the changing character of tenancy relations with the organized movement of the tenants (as under the O.B. programme) would be to compare the tenancy relations that these two types of tenants (recorded and unrecorded) are involved in with their respective landlords. This is precisely what we intend to do in the present chapter and the next. Specifically, we would like to know to what extent the recorded tenants differ from the unrecorded ones in respect of class-caste-social background, motivations for leasing-in land, terms and conditions of lease contracts faced by them, crop and cost-sharing patterns, and so on. In order to focus the impact of changing levels of agricultural technology on tenancy structure, we may observe the tenancy situations prevailing over the 'advanced' and the 'backward' regions of our study area. Briefly, we will discuss two 'regions' which we have demarcated out of twelve surveyed villages in four blocks in the district of Midnapore. Region I represents, by the state's own norms, a relatively 'advanced' area in terms of irrigation base, particularly with the availability of water from public irrigation systems (deep tube-well and river-lift) and canals. Region II, again in terms of local standards, is relatively 'backward' with very little support from the public irrigation system; the private tubewells owned and operated by a very small percentage of cultivators are not adequate to meet the irrigation requirements of the large mass of cultivators, who cannot afford tube-well irrigation.

---

[4] The tenancy relations of the unrecorded tenants are traditional in the sense that they enjoy no protection from upward revision of rent by their landlords and no security of tenure and as such may be evicted at-will by the landlords.

In this chapter, we will first examine the socio-economic status of the two categories of tenants in the regions surveyed.[5] We then examine who form the group of lessors and what their socio-economic background is. More specifically, the question studied is: who leases from whom? The motivations for leasing in as well as the choice of contractual form (crop-sharing, fixed-rent tenancy and so on) are explained, followed by a discussion on some other issues such as differentiation of the tenants on the basis of a mode of labour utilization/exploitation and tenants' involvement in the land market as purchasers and/or sellers of land. The remaining issues relating to the changing terms and conditions of tenancy contracts and tenurial relations following political mobilization and organization of the tenantry in West Bengal will be discussed in the next chapter.

Socio-economic Status of Tenant Households

In order to understand the socio-economic status of the tenant households, we may consider the distribution of their ownership and operational holdings. While the distribution of ownership holdings would reveal the position of these households in the land-owning hierarchy, the size of operational holdings would represent their status as cultivators and their access to land and, more specifically, their earning capabilities and employment potential are determined by operational holdings.

Ownership Distribution: The data on ownership holdings of the two categories of tenants in our survey regions are presented in Table 4.1. A few important points emerging from the table are as follows:

---

[5] Some scholars argue that the socio-economic status of tenants vis-à-vis landlords reflects their respective bargaining strength. Thus the caste background and land possessed by them are taken cognizance of to form an idea about their respective bargaining strength. See Bharadwaj and Das (1975); Murty (1987: A111–A120). While these factors need not be rejected as indicative of the bargaining position of the two parties, we emphasize that this is also determined by their relative organizational strength. On this count, our hypothesis has been that as an organised campaign (such as O.B.) is launched in West Bengal, even the tenants of lower caste/class status may add to their bargaining strength, thereby altering the overall traditional tenurial relations.

Table 4.1
Land-ownership Status of Unrecorded and Recorded Tenants

Region	Size Group (in acres)	No. of households	Owned area (in acres)	Average size (in acres)
A. UNRECORDED TENANTS				
I	0.00	–	–	–
	0.01–0.99	27 (42.2)	11.65 (11.2)	0.43
	1.00–2.49	22 (34.4)	32.40 (31.1)	1.47
	2.50–4.99	12 (18.8)	42.14 (40.4)	3.51
	5.00 and above	3 (4.6)	18.08 (17.3)	6.03
	All sizes	64 (100.0)	104.27 (100.0)	1.93
II	0.00	2 (3.5)	–	–
	0.01–0.99	32 (56.1)	12.15 (19.6)	0.38
	1.00–2.49	16 (28.1)	22.17 (35.7)	1.39
	2.50–4.99	5 (8.8)	15.87 (25.6)	3.17
	5.00 and above	2 (3.5)	11.84 (19.1)	5.92
	All sizes	57 (100.0)	62.03 (100.0)	1.09
B. RECORDED TENANTS				
I	0.00	1 (1.8)	–	–
	0.01–0.99	28 (50.0)	13.44 (14.8)	0.48
	1.00–2.49	15 (26.8)	23.51 (25.8)	1.57
	2.50–4.99	8 (14.3)	29.56 (32.5)	3.70
	5.00 and above	4 (7.1)	24.48 (26.9)	6.12
	All sizes	56 (100.0)	90.99 (100.0)	1.62
II	0.00	2 (4.3)	–	–
	0.01–0.99	28 (56.6)	10.47 (23.2)	0.37
	1.00–2.49	13 (27.7)	21.56 (47.8)	1.66
	2.50–4.99	4 (8.5)	13.10 (29.0)	3.28
	5.00 and above	–	–	–
	All sizes	47 (100.0)	45.13 (100.0)	0.96

Note: Figures in the parentheses are percentages of the total.

First, there are very few pure tenants in the regions studied by us. Only two out of 121 unrecorded tenants and three out of 103 recorded tenants fall in the category of zero land-owning tenants. This means that the majority of our tenant households actually belong to the category of owner-cum-tenants. Such a low incidence of pure tenancy in our study area is perhaps an indication of lessors' preference for those tenants who have some land of their own instead of those who otherwise operate largely as agricultural labourers. Presumably, the lessor believes that a tenant with some land of his own, and by implication with the adequate experience of farming, would prove a better tenant, at least in terms of providing a better security for obtaining rent from the side of the lessor.[6] It is also possible in the context of West Bengal that many of the erstwhile landless tenants might have been elevated to the class of owner-cum-tenants with the distribution of vested agricultural land among them in recent years, which has caused a very low incidence of pure tenancy.

Second, it is clear that a large majority of the tenants (both unrecorded and recorded) belong to ownership categories of less than 2.5 acres, with even greater concentration in the category representing less than 1.00 acre.[7] As observed in Table 4.1, among the unrecorded tenants nearly 77 per cent in Region I and 88 per cent in Region II owned land less than 2.5 acres each. The corresponding figures for the recorded tenants in the two regions are nearly 78 per cent and 88 per cent respectively. All these seem to indicate that constrained by inadequate land at their disposal, these households look for some opening in the land-lease market, the terms of lease notwithstanding.

Third, the possibility of some tenants being drawn from higher ownership categories is slightly greater in agriculturally developed region compared to that in the backward region. This is true for both the unrecorded and the recorded tenants. As is clear from the table, while about 23 per cent of the unrecorded tenants and 21 per cent of the recorded tenants in Region I belong to higher ownership size groups of above 2.50 acres, the corresponding figures for the two groups of tenants in Region II are 12 per cent and 9 per cent respectively. This provides some support to the view often put forward that with the advancement of agriculture even the owners of higher categories might enter the land-lease market so as to augment their scale of cultivation further and reap fuller benefits of improved agricultural technology.

[6] In their study of some Orissa villages, Bharadwaj and Das (1975: 230) note 'security of obtaining rent' as the reason provided by the lessors preferring landed to landless tenants.

[7] The fact that the majority of tenants in our sample belong to ownership categories of less than 2.50 acres is very much consistent with the overall tenancy structure prevailing in West Bengal today as we have observed in Chapter 3.

Operational holdings: Information on tenants' operational holdings is presented in Table 4.2 for the unrecorded and the recorded tenants, respectively. We consider the distribution of operational holdings separately for the two cropping seasons, namely Kharif and Rabi/Boro.[8] The distribution of operational holdings reveals a picture broadly similar to that noted earlier for the ownership holdings. Thus the vast majority of the tenants (both unrecorded and recorded) belong to the categories of cultivators operating less than 2.5 acres of land in both the regions. The overall distribution pattern of tenant operational holdings thus indicates preponderance of households with very low cultivating status in the land-lease market. Further, no appreciable difference is discernible in this context between the two categories of tenants. In other words, for a big majority of tenants, the pattern of distribution of their operational holdings does not show a marked difference between the recorded and the unrecorded categories. In terms of their operational area status, both groups seem to enjoy an almost identical economic status, all along the farm size continuum.

This is, however, not to deny that a higher percentage of tenants belonging to higher size groups is greater in agriculturally progressive Region I compared to those in the backward Region II. As observed from Table 4.2, while nearly 30 per cent of the unrecorded tenants operate more than 2.50 acres of land in Region I, the corresponding percentage in Region II is only 15 per cent. The picture is almost the same in the case of the recorded tenants. The percentage of recorded tenants cultivating more than 2.50 acres of land is nearly 29 per cent in Region I but a mere 11 per cent in Region II. All these facts reinforce our earlier observation that with the arrival of improved agricultural technology, more and more cultivators of higher sizes are likely to be drawn as lessees in the land-lease market primarily in their pursuit of extending the scale of cultivation, *inter alia*, to spread the cost of indivisibilities over a large quantum of output.

---

[8] This is essential because the leasing pattern changes from one cropping season to the other. Thus if a household leases in more land in one particular season compared to the other, not only he be elevated to higher economic status but it may also add to his bargaining power. In our subsequent discussion, however, for analytical reasons, we consider operational area during the dominant Kharif season as the index of household's overall economic status.

Table 4.2
Operational Holdings and Area Operated by Unrecorded and Recorded Tenants

Region	Size Group (in acres)	Kharif season			Rabi/Boro season		
		No. of holdings	Area (in acres)	Av. op. area	No. of holdings	Area (in acres)	Av. op. area
A. Unrecorded Tenants							
I	0.01–0.99	29 (45.3)	16.2 (14.1)	0.56	18 (28.1)	11.4 (8.7)	0.63
	1.00–2.49	16 (25.0)	28.3 (25.2)	1.77	24 (37.5)	36.7 (28.2)	1.53
	2.50–4.99	17 (26.6)	56.3 (50.2)	3.31	21 (32.8)	77.0 (59.2)	3.67
	5.00 and above	2 (3.1)	11.4 (10.2)	5.70	1 (1.6)	5.0 (3.8)	5.00
	All sizes	64 (100.0)	112.2 (100.0)	1.75	64 (100.0)	130.1 (100.0)	2.03
II	0.01–0.99	23 (40.4)	14.1 (16.8)	0.61	23 (40.4)	13.7 (17.3)	0.60
	1.00–2.49	26 (45.6)	38.6 (45.9)	1.48	27 (47.4)	39.6 (49.7)	1.47
	2.50–4.99	6 (10.5)	20.7 (24.6)	3.44	6 (10.5)	20.8 (26.2)	3.47
	5.00 and above	2 (3.5)	10.8 (12.8)	5.38	1 (1.8)	5.4 (6.8)	5.40
	All sizes	57 (100.0)	84.2 (100.0)	1.47	57 (100.0)	79.5 (100.0)	1.40
B. Recorded Tenants							
I	0.01–0.99	11 (19.6)	6.8 (5.9)	0.62	11 (19.6)	7.8 (6.6)	0.71
	1.00–2.49	29 (51.8)	42.0 (36.2)	1.45	28 (50.0)	39.5 (33.6)	1.41
	2.50–4.99	11 (19.6)	37.5 (32.4)	3.41	12 (21.4)	41.1 (34.9)	3.43
	5.00 and above	5 (8.9)	29.7 (25.5)	5.94	5 (8.9)	29.2 (24.8)	5.85
	All sizes	56 (100.0)	116.0 (100.0)	2.07	56 (100.0)	117.6 (100.0)	2.10
II	0.01–0.99	25 (53.2)	14.4 (24.1)	0.57	27 (57.5)	14.7 (27.8)	0.54
	1.00–2.49	17 (36.2)	29.0 (48.7)	1.70	18 (38.3)	32.4 (61.4)	1.80
	2.50–4.99	5 (10.6)	16.2 (27.2)	3.24	2 (4.2)	5.7 (10.8)	2.86
	5.00 and above	–	–	–	–	–	–
	All sizes	47 (100.0)	59.6 (100.0)	1.27	47 (100.0)	52.8 (100.0)	1.12

As regards the distribution of operational holdings of the tenants between the two seasons, not much difference seems to exist between the regions. This is more or less true of both categories of tenants. The only noticeable departure in this regard is that, in the agriculturally progressive Region I, a section of the unrecorded tenants of lower size groups, particularly those belonging to less than 1.0 acre and 1.0–2.49 acres categories, leased in more land during the Boro season and accordingly moved to the higher size groups of operational holdings.[9] This means that there is a greater preference among the households in lower categories to lease in more land or to enter into fresh tenancy arrangement during the Boro season which, in real terms, provides opportunities for culti-vation under better technological conditions. In some cases, such leases are obtained as part of interlocked contracts, particularly between land-lease and labour.[10] From the viewpoint of the land-owner, by leasing out a fraction of his cultivable land during the Boro season, not only does he earn an assured rent but, more importantly, it assures him a degree of labour supply through his tenant(s) for crucial field crop operations (such as, sowing and harvesting) in the cultivation of his self-operated land. This apart, there is also a general tendency among the landowners to enter the lease market preferably during the Boro season in order to evade the provision of tenancy act which allows the tenant to record in his name the tenanted portion of land. In as much as there is lesser fear of land being recorded in the names of tenants if leased out exclusively for the Boro season[11] and that some landowners also prefer earning an assured rental while avoiding the difficulty of self-cultivation, such a tendency is likely to increase in the years to come increasingly lending a seasonal character to tenancy in West Bengal.

[9] This is quite contrary to the situation reported by Bandyopadhyay (1975) from a region at the Hoogly-Burdwan border in West Bengal where large 'enterprising' farmers leased in huge land during Boro season to do cultivation on commercial basis.

[10] We shall devote greater attention to interlocked market transactions in the next chapter.

[11] During our field survey, we discovered that there was complete unanimity among the sample tenants that none of them would go in for recording if the land was leased in for Boro season only. This means that these contracts are purely seasonal and the tenants voluntarily give back their leased-in plots to the landlords at the end of the season.

Social status: Some idea about the social status of the tenant households can be obtained by looking at their caste-wise distribution and the level of education. The data on caste composition of the tenant households (Table 4.3) reveal that very few of the tenant households in our sample area belong to the most superior caste group namely, 'Brahmin/Baishnab'. A significant number of tenants particularly the unrecorded ones, belong to the 'Caste Hindu' category, the majority of whom are actually drawn from *Mahisya* caste who are considered the cultivating community in the district. As between the two categories of tenants, the recorded ones have a much higher percentage of lower caste/tribals. The fact that a greater percentage of the recorded tenants in our sample belong to the lower rank in the caste hierarchy implies a weaker social status for them compared with their unrecorded counterpart.

Table 4.3
Caste Status of Tenant Households: Two Regions Combined (Percentages)

Caste	Unrecorded tenants	Recorded tenants	All tenants
Brahmin/Baishnab	4.13	0.97	2.68
Caste Hindu	67.77	39.81	54.91
Lower Caste & Tribal	27.27	59.22	41.96
Mohammedan	0.83	–	0.45
Total	100.00	100.00	100.00
	(121)	(103)	(224)

Note: Figures in parentheses indicate total number of sample households.

As regards the level of education (see Appendix Table A5), the level of absolute illiteracy is very low for all categories of tenants in our study area. However, comparing the two categories of tenants, it appears that the level of illiteracy is relatively higher among the recorded tenants. Another important point to note is that a larger proportion of literates among all categories of tenants failed to go beyond middle-level education. In brief, our data clearly bring out the fact that compared with the unrecorded tenants, the recorded tenants have a lower percentage of literates and higher percentage of lower caste/tribal households. In other words, in general, the recorded tenants have a relatively inferior social status.

While examining the social status of the tenant households, it may be of some interest to take note of their own past occupation as also their ancestral occupations. In this context, our study presents some interesting features (Table 4.4). It appears that compared with the recorded tenants, a relatively higher percentage of the unrecorded tenants reported self-cultivation as having been their main occupation earlier. On the other hand, the percentage of households belonging to erstwhile agricultural labour families have been higher in the case of recorded tenants. Actually, these are the households which, apart from depending mostly on the sale of their labour, cultivated some leased in land which was later recorded in their very names. The tendency for more of the recorded tenants to be drawn from agricultural labour households becomes sharper if we examine the distribution of all tenants according to their ancestral occupations. The incidence of the tenant's father having worked as an agricultural labourer is much higher in the case of recorded tenants compared to unrecorded ones.

Table 4.4
Previous Work Description and Ancestral Occupation of Tenant Households: Two Regions Combined (Percentages)

Item	Unrecorded tenants	Recorded tenants	All tenants
Earlier Occupation of the tenant:			
(a) Self-cultivation	71.08	65.05	68.30
(b) Agricultural labour	26.44	33.98	29.91
(c) Non-agricultural work	2.48	0.97	1.79
Occupation of tenant's father:			
(a) Self-cultivation	72.73	55.34	64.73
(b) Agricultural labour	22.31	39.81	30.36
(c) Non-Agricultural work	4.96	4.85	4.91

Another interesting aspect of the difference in the background of the two types of tenants is brought out by their distribution according to the period of involvement in leasing in practices. As is evident from Table 4.5, considering both regions together, nearly 42 per cent of the unrecorded tenants entered the land-lease market only during the past two to five years. In sharp contrast, in the case of recorded tenants, nearly 96 per cent of them have been in the

Table 4.5

Period of Involvement in Leasing-in Practices: Two Regions Combined (Percentages)

Period of involvement	Unrecorded tenants	Recorded tenants	All tenants
More than 25 years	15.70	52.43	32.59
16–25 years	14.88	30.10	21.88
11–15 years	10.74	13.59	12.05
6–10 years	13.22	2.91	8.48
2–5 years	42.98	0.97	23.66
1 year	1.65	–	0.89
One season	0.83	–	0.45

land-lease market for as many as fifteen years, so much so that even the percentage of those involved in leasing in land for twenty-five years or more turns out to be no less than 52 per cent. This means that while a majority of the recorded tenants traditionally belong to the class of sharecropper-cum-agricultural labourers, the unrecorded tenants are the relatively new entrants who have been attracted to leasing in land only in recent years. The point to note in this context is that such tenants in our study area do not necessarily come from the class of large cultivators; rather, a majority of them belong to lower size-groups of holdings (mostly less than 2.5 acres with greater concentration in the category representing less than 1.0 acre).

Who are the Lessors?

We now proceed to find out who the lessors are in our study area. More specifically, who leases from whom? One way of examining this question could have been to establish contact with the lessor households specific to our tenant households and then obtain information on their socio-economic status, motivation and preference for leasing out, etc. However, to our disappointment, this procedure did not work effectively largely due to the proverbial unwillingness of such households to disclose their status as lessors, as we have reported in Appendix I. The best alternative available to us was, therefore, to enquire about the area owned, caste, occupation, etc. of the lessors from the sample tenants themselves. To be quite sure about the authenticity of this crucial agrarian feature, the information thus obtained from the tenants was thoroughly cross-checked with other knowledgeable persons in the village. This process is also facilitated particularly when more than one tenant leased in land from a common lessor. In a technical sense, our procedure would appear to be only the second best, yet, in terms of reliability of information, it has much to commend itself. It is almost certain that a lessor talking about himself would be much less reliable than a lessee talking about his lessor, especially when two or more lessees are talking about the very same individual lessor.

On this basis, we present in Table 4.6 data on the distribution of lease units by lessee-lessor groups. What we actually intend here is to find out which class of lessees (tenants) lease in land from which class of lessors (landlords). Thus we distribute the lessors specific to each category of lessees into different ownership groups. The lessors are distributed over five ownership groups: (*a*) less than 1.0 acre (lower marginal); (*b*) 1.0–2.49 acres (upper marginal); (*c*) 2.50–4.99 acres (small); (*d*) 5.00–9.99 acres (medium); and (*e*) 10.0 acres and above (big).

It is evident from Table 4.6 that the lessors of the unrecorded lessees come from all size groups of ownership holdings in Region I although there seems to operate a slightly greater concentration in 'small' and 'middle' land-owning categories. The picture is similar in Region II, the only difference being that there are very few lessors in the ownership group of 10.0 acres and above. Another important feature of the lease arrangements is that there is a tendency, though not decisive, of smaller unrecorded lessees leasing in land more from the smaller lessors while the bigger unrecorded lessees being preferred by the bigger lessors. In the case of unrecorded lessees, in the category of less than 1.0 acre in Region I, nearly 21 per cent of their lessors belong to 'lower marginal' land-owning category while only about 10 per cent of them fall in 'big' category. On the other hand, for the lessees in the category of 2.50–4.99 acres, only about 9 per cent of the lessors are from 'lower marginal' category against nearly 20 per cent in 'big' category. An almost similar tendency is discernible in Region II if we restrict our comparison between the lessors owning less than 10.0 acres and their lessees. On the whole, it is fairly obvious that although

Table 4.6

Distribution of Lease Units by Lessee-Lessor Groups

Region	Operational holding of lessees (in acres)	No. of tenants	Ownership holding of lessors (percentage)					Total	Lease contracts per lessee
			Less than 1.00	1.00 to 2.49	2.50 to 4.99	5.00 to 9.99	10.00 and above		
A. UNRECORDED LESSEES									
I	Less than 1.00	28	21.43	19.05	26.19	23.81	9.52	100.00 (42)	1.50
	1.00–2.49	17	18.60	23.26	16.27	23.26	18.61	100.00 (43)	2.53
	2.50–4.99	17	8.57	20.00	28.57	22.85	20.01	100.00 (35)	2.06
	5.00 & above	2	–	–	–	33.33	66.67	100.00 (3)	1.50
	All sizes	64	16.24	20.33	22.76	23.58	17.09	100.00 (123)	1.92
II	Less than 1.00	21	12.28	29.82	45.61	8.77	3.52	100.00 (57)	2.71
	1.00–2.49	27	19.67	29.51	36.07	13.11	1.64	100.00 (61)	2.26
	2.50–4.99	6	44.45	11.11	22.22	22.22	–	100.00 (9)	1.50
	5.00 & above	3	–	20.00	40.00	40.00	–	100.00 (5)	1.67
	All sizes	57	17.42	28.03	39.39	12.88	2.28	100.00 (132)	2.32
B. RECORDED LESSEES									
I	Less than 1.00	11	–	6.25	25.00	31.25	37.50	100.00 (16)	1.45
	1.00–2.49	29	6.82	11.36	11.36	25.00	45.46	100.00 (44)	1.52
	2.50–4.99	11	5.88	23.23	11.76	29.41	29.41	100.00 (17)	1.55
	5.00 & above	5	–	–	–	33.33	66.67	100.00 (6)	1.20
	All sizes	56	4.82	12.05	13.25	27.71	42.17	100.00 (83)	1.48
II	Less than 1.00	24	11.11	25.00	16.67	8.33	38.89	100.00 (36)	1.50
	1.00–2.49	18	6.25	28.13	12.50	18.74	34.38	100.00 (32)	1.78
	2.50–4.99	5	–	–	16.67	50.00	33.33	100.00 (6)	1.20
	5.00 & above	0	–	–	–	–	–	–	–
	All sizes	47	8.11	24.32	14.86	16.22	39.49	100.00 (74)	1.57

the lessors of the unrecorded lessees come from all sizes of farms all along the ownership continuum, yet there seems to be a tendency among the bigger lessors to prefer unrecorded lessees with higher cultivating status and smaller lessors going in for lessees of lower order. This trend is relatively more pronounced in the agriculturally progressive Region I.[12]

The situation is different in the case of recorded lessees, as more of their lessors come from the higher ownership categories. It is evident from Table 4.6 that the highest percentage of the lessors of the recorded lessees of almost all size groups belong to the 'big' land-owning category in both the regions. It, however, needs to be mentioned that even in the case of recorded lessees, the percentage of lessors in 'upper marginal', 'small' and 'medium' land-owning categories have not been altogether insignificant. However, as all categories of recorded tenants have leased in more from the lessors of the higher order, no clear association can be insisted upon between the cultivating status of the recorded lessees and ownership status of their lessors.

In Table 4.6, we have also given information on the number of lessors/lease contracts per lessee of various size groups. Several important features emerge in this context. First, the number of lease contracts per lessee exceeds 1.0 for all types of unrecorded and recorded lessees in both the regions.[13] This implies that there is no one-to-one tie-up of the lessee to specific lessor. In fact, all types of lessees are now free to lease in from as many lessors as they are willing to or can afford to, given their own resource endowment. Leasing in land from more than one lessor provides an opportunity to the lessee not only to augment his operated area but often to avail of the benefit of cultivating lands of various grades which provides a greater degree of economic security,

[12] Bharadwaj and Das (1975: 230) also notice such a tendency of bigger lessors leasing out to relatively better-off tenants in some irrigated villages in Orissa. The situation observed by us is, however, somewhat different from what is observed in another study on Nadia district of West Bengal where big landowners among lessors are conspicuous by their almost complete absence. See Ray (1978: A121).

[13] The fact that the number of lease contracts per lessee far exceeds 1.0 in both of our regions should not be interpreted that the lessors are more in number than the lessees. In fact it is found that just as a lessee very often leases in land from more than one lessor, the latter too frequently leases out small parcels to more than one lessee. This is one of the reasons for the number of lessors to exceed the number of lessees in our table.

especially in a production regime characterized by a low level of irrigation development. From the side of the lessor, this might mean adopting a policy of parcellization so as to extract greater effort per unit of land from every lessee and/or bargaining for a higher rental share under a crop-sharing system.

Second, the number of lease contracts per lessee is greater for the lessees of lower size groups. This can be interpreted in terms of our previous argument of lessors and lessees setting their respective strategies of maximizing earnings. Thus while leasing in from a number of lessors may enable a section of land-scarce but labour-abundant tenant families to attempt better utilization of their family resources (most importantly, labour power), the lessors also get an opportunity of extracting maximum gain (in terms of shareable output) by indirectly forcing such tenants to put maximum effort on the land leased out by them.[14]

Third, between the two types of lessees, the unrecorded ones have higher number of lease contract per lessee in both the regions. This means that the unrecorded lessees in both the regions have been able to establish rapport with a greater number of lessors.[15] The latter too would accord special preference to the unrecorded tenants who, in the perception of the lessors, are more 'trustworthy'.

We have also information on the occupational status of the lessors of the sample lessees. Table 4.7 shows that a fairly high percentage of the lessors of the unrecorded lessees have self-cultivation as the main occupation. Among the primarily non-cultivating lessors, the majority are in service which is followed by the lessors engaged in trade and business. An almost similar picture is obtained in the case of the lessors of the recorded lessees. However, a strict comparison of the two categories of lessees reveals that the percentage of non-cultivating interests among the lessors is relatively higher in the case of the recorded lessees compared with the unrecorded lessees. The majority of these lessors are engaged in occupations such as service and business/

[14] Bharadwaj and Das (1975: 225) interpret this as a method of extracting an additional element of 'hidden rent' by the landlords from their tenants with larger families.

[15] This does not necessarily mean that the proportion of leased-in area to operated area has been higher in the case of unrecorded lessees compared to recorded ones. In fact, it is the other way round in most cases. This would become clear when we discuss below the incidence of leasing in land by various categories of lessees.

Table 4.7
Principal Occupation of Lessors to Sample Lessees: Two Regions Combined

Operational holding of lessees (in acres)	Occupation of lessors (percentage)				
	Self-culti-vation	Service	Trade/ Business	Widow/ Disabled	Other non-agril. activities
A. UNRECORDED LESSEES					
Less than 1.00	48.48	30.30	10.10	2.02	9.09
1.00–2.49	44.22	33.65	13.46	2.88	5.77
2.50–4.99	34.09	43.18	18.18	–	4.54
5.00 & above	37.50	50.00	12.50	–	–
All sizes	43.92	34.51	12.94	1.96	6.67
B. RECORDED LESSEES					
Less than 1.00	42.30	28.85	23.08	–	5.77
1.00–2.49	38.67	29.33	17.33	5.33	9.33
2.50–4.99	29.17	25.00	25.00	4.17	16.67
5.00 & above	33.33	50.00	16.67	–	–
All sizes	38.22	29.30	20.38	3.18	8.92

trade and a few of them are widows/disabled. On the whole, it appears that primarily non-agricultural land-owning households which have only a secondary interest in land suffered relatively more through barga recording in our study area. Another interesting feature emerging from Table 4.7 is that the lessees in smaller size groups tend to lease in more from the lessors who also belong to the cultivating community. On the other hand, primarily non-cultivating categories (such as those in service and trade/business) while leasing out their land generally prefer lessees of higher size groups. This tendency seems to be relatively more distinct in the case of the lessors of the unrecorded lessees.

Data on the caste status of the lessors are given in Table 4.8. It may be seen that the percentage of the lessors belonging to superior caste category namely, 'Brahmin/Baishnab' has been quite high, particularly in comparison to what we have earlier observed for the lessees. A substantial number of the lessors of all types of lessees also belong to the 'Caste Hindu' category, while the percentage of 'Lower Caste and Tribals' is not very high among them. The overall picture of caste-distribution of lessors seems to indicate that they enjoy a superior social status compared to their own tenants.

Table 4.8

Caste Status of Lessors to Sample Lessees: Two Regions Combined (Percentages)

Caste	Unrecorded lessees	Recorded lessees	All lessees
Brahmin/Baishnab	20.23	16.95	18.99
Caste Hindu	71.98	78.02	74.52
Lower Caste & Tribal	7.00	4.40	6.01
Mohammedan	0.79	0.63	0.48

Incidence of Land-leasing and Types of Tenancy

The incidence of leasing in land is unlikely to be the same for tenants of all size groups. To examine whether the incidence of leasing in varies across farm size continuum, we present in Table 4.9 information on the percentage of leased in area to operated area respectively for the unrecorded and the recorded tenants of different size groups. A number of points need to be underlined. First, during the Kharif season, the percentage of leased in area to operated area does not seem to differ strikingly among the unrecorded tenants of various size groups in the agriculturally progressive Region I. In the relatively backward Region II, although smaller holdings show a tendency to lease in more land, the relationship is not very systematic. In any case, the overall pattern of leasing in land by the unrecorded tenants of different size groups during the Kharif season does not help establish a clear relationship between size of tenant operational holding and proportion of area actually leased in.

The situation, however, changes markedly during the Rabi/Boro season. In this season, in the agriculturally progressive Region I, not only do the unrecorded tenants of all size groups report a higher percentage of leased in area but the households in the lower size groups clearly reveal a greater tendency towards leasing in more land. In Region II, although the percentage of leased in area during the Boro/Rabi season declines practically for all categories of unrecorded tenants, those falling in the category of less than 1.0 acre seem to be quite successful in leasing in more area. All these facts strengthen two of our earlier observations namely that there has been a growing tendency towards the functioning of the lease market for land at greater scale during the Boro/Rabi season and that the tenant households in lower size groups obtained precedence in this regard.

Coming now to the recorded tenants, it is evident that in the lower size groups, they have a greater percentage of leased in area in both the regions and for both the seasons. An important difference between the two types of tenants has been that, contrary to the case of unrecorded tenants, the recorded ones, practically from all size groups, report higher percentage of leased in area to operated area during the Kharif season. This means that the recorded tenants have a lower proportion of owned area under cultivation and as such their position is closer to the predominantly sharecropper families. The proportion of leased in area, however, declines for almost all size groups of recorded tenants during the Boro season. This is possible if the tenants fail to continue with the cultivation of their entire recorded land during the Boro season while at the same time being unsuccessful in entering into a fresh tenancy arrangement for this season. Although some of the recorded tenants in Region I, particularly those falling in the category of less than 1.0 acre, have been successful in making fresh tenancy arrangement during Boro season, there has been a general tendency among the landowners to prefer, even for seasonal arrangements, those tenants who earlier proved their trustworthiness by not recording their names against the land leased in during the past from other landowners. This, however, does not mean that the recorded tenants have been altogether unsuccessful in entering into such seasonal tenancy contracts. The point to emphasize is that the landowners tend to reveal a differential preference in the matter of choosing their tenants even for seasonal contracts in the face of 'fear of recording'.

Types of tenancy: Table 4.9 also provides information on the proportion of leased in area under different tenancy arrangements. It is fairly obvious that sharecropping has been unequivocally the dominant form of tenancy both for the unrecorded and the recorded tenants, particularly during the Kharif season. Although some of the recorded tenants are reported to have leased in some land under fixed produce contract in Region I, the predominance of share-crop tenancy is clearly established in the Kharif season.

Table 4.9
Distribution of Leased-in Land by Types of Tenancy

Size Group (in acres)	Percentage of leased in area to operated area		Kharif season — Proportion of leased in area under			Rabi/Boro season — Proportion of leased in area under		
	Kharif season	Rabi/Boro season	Crop-sharing	Fixed produce contract	Fixed cash contract	Crop-sharing	Fixed produce contract	Fixed cash contract
A. UNRECORDED TENANTS								
Region I								
0.01–0.99	29.38	59.38	100.00	–	–	58.01	41.99	–
1.00–2.49	31.06	42.51	100.00	–	–	79.70	16.46	3.84
2.50–4.99	26.66	34.27	93.79	4.77	1.44	59.21	39.05	1.74
5.00 & above	30.70	32.00	100.00	–	–	100.00	–	–
All sizes	28.48	38.70	97.07	2.12	0.81	66.28	31.20	2.52
Region II								
0.01–0.99	52.80	73.78	100.00	–	–	97.63	1.38	0.99
1.00–2.49	41.39	34.84	100.00	–	–	97.52	0.89	1.59
2.50–4.99	11.43	22.22	100.00	–	–	93.52	6.48	–
5.00 & above	60.41	7.41	100.00	–	–	100.00	–	–
All sizes	38.38	36.39	100.00	–	–	96.62	2.28	1.10
B. RECORDED TENANTS								
Region I								
0.01–0.99	53.72	86.86	93.02	6.98	–	94.71	5.29	–
1.00–2.49	53.84	49.73	84.95	13.73	1.32	66.30	32.89	0.81

2.50–4.99	38.74	46.98	91.84	8.16	—	74.33	25.67	—
5.00 & above	21.73	20.55	100.00	—	—	100.00	—	—
All sizes	40.73	44.00	89.29	9.95	0.76	76.94	22.75	0.31
Region II								
0.01–0.99	62.40	52.52	98.40	—	1.68	93.51	—	6.49
1.00–2.49	30.65	27.22	100.00	—	—	96.40	3.60	—
2.50–4.99	26.82	2.79	100.00	—	—	100.00	—	—
5.00 & above	—	—	—	—	—	—	—	—
All sizes	37.26	30.65	99.31	—	0.69	95.20	1.80	3.00

Some deviation from this situation is discernible during the Boro/ Rabi season. In this season, both the unrecorded and the recorded tenants in the agriculturally advanced Region I lease in some land under fixed produce contracts. As is evident from Table 4.9, the percentage of leased in area under fixed produce contracts is nearly 31 per cent for the unrecorded tenants and about 23 per cent for the recorded tenants in Region I. In the relatively backward Region II, however, share-crop tenancy continues to predominate for both types of tenants during the Boro season. It seems that fixed rent tenancy is a newly emerging category in some areas, mostly under the impact of new agricultural technology.

Another noticeable fact is that among the unrecorded tenants in Region I, those operating land less than 1.0 acre tend to lease in more land under fixed produce contract during the Boro season. The next to follow are those in the size group 2.50–4.99 acres. Among the recorded tenants in Region I, those operating 1.0–2.49 acres report highest percentage of leased in area under fixed rent contract during the Boro season followed by the tenants in the group 2.50–4.99. Both the unrecorded and the recorded tenants operating 5.0 acres and above, however, prefer to lease in completely under crop-sharing contracts even during the Boro season. Thus, in our study area, the overall picture seems to suggest that the incidence of leasing in more land under fixed produce contract during the Boro season has been higher among the lower categories of tenants.

Crop-wise distribution of lease contracts: The foregoing discussion tends to give the impression that only fixed-rent tenancy has gained predominance in agriculturally progressive region during the Boro/Rabi season. It is, however, not yet fully clear which of the crop/crops promote fixed-rent tenancy. In order to fill up this gap, we also analysed crop-wise distribution of lease contracts under crop-sharing and fixed-rent tenancy in our study area.

The crop-wise distribution of tenancy arrangements (see Appendix Table A6) reveals that crop-sharing tenancy predominates in the case of the principal crop of the area, that is, Aman paddy, for both types of tenants as well as for both the sample regions. The situation, however, changes expectedly in the Boro/Rabi season. Thus for Boro paddy, the most important crop of this season, a considerable number of lease units are found to be under fixed-rent tenancy particularly in the agriculturally progressive Region I.

Another noticeable fact is that the incidence of lease units being under fixed rent contract for Boro paddy has been much higher in the case of unrecorded tenants compared with the recorded ones.[16] Thus, out of a total of seventy-one cases under which Boro paddy is cultivated by the unrecorded tenants in Region I, in twenty-six cases the arrangements are on fixed rent contract. In the case of the recorded tenants of the same region, in six out of forty-six cases there were fixed-rent arrangements for Boro paddy. As regards fixed-rent cases in different size groups of holdings, we observe that fixed-rent tenancy in the case of Boro paddy is preferred more by the tenants in the lower farm size groups. This is consistent with our earlier observation that there is a higher incidence of fixed-rented acreage in the smaller size-groups of tenants in our study area. Some explanations concerning the greater preference for fixed-rent contract among the tenants in the lower categories have been attempted earlier. In the specific case of the tenants cultivating Boro paddy, many of them actually belong to predominantly agricultural labour families who enter into fresh tenancy arrangement on seasonal basis for this crop alone, often as a part of an interlinked land-lease and labour contract.

As regards other cash crops cultivated during the Boro/Rabi season, no definite picture is discernible. Thus, while sharecropping predominates in the case of potato in both the regions and for both types of tenants, fixed-rent contract assumes prevalence in the case of another cash crop namely, 'karala'.[17] For other crops such as sugarcane and Aus paddy, again sharecropping appears as the dominant form of tenancy.

Farm Family Resources and Tenancy

We have noted (in Chapter 1) the various explanations for the persistence of tenancy in general and share-crop tenancy in particular. We found that a powerful explanation of the persistence of tenancy has been the non-existence of markets or imperfect tradeability of certain input factors.[18] It is argued that in an agrarian

---

[16] For Boro paddy, fixed rent means fixed produce payable after the harvest by the tenant.

[17] For 'karala', tenancy actually takes the form of fixed cash rent contract whereby the tenants pay a fixed sum in advance to the landowners.

[18] For details see Chapter 1 above.

economy with an underdeveloped labour market, the households with higher labour-land ratio might involve themselves in leasing in land in their attempt to mitigate the effects of labour market uncertainty. In the same way, imperfect marketability of factors such as draught power and other agricultural implements may also induce a section of peasants to enter into tenancy contracts.

In this section, we examine the extent to which the endowment of farm family resources determine the incidence of leasing in land in our study area. In order to examine the impact of the household's resource endowment on the extent of land-leasing, we consider three variables: (a) owned cultivated area per family worker; (b) the value of draught animals per family worker; and (c) the value of farm machinery per family worker. In other words, all these variables indicate the household's endowment of land and capital resources in relation to its available labour power in the family. What we do here is first divide the tenant households into various groups depending upon the proportion of leased in area to total operated area,[19] and then calculate the mean values of these variables for each group of tenants. The main objective is to see whether the households reporting higher percentage of leased in area to total operated area also possess a greater endowment of these resources.

Table 4.10 presents the distribution of the two groups of tenants (unrecorded and recorded) according to the proportion of leased in area to their total operated area and provide data on their respective resource endowments. It is evident from the table that, among the three variables representing the households' resource endowments, owned cultivated land per family worker appears to be the most important determinant of the extent of leasing in (measured in terms of the ratio of area leased in to operated area) for both the unrecorded and the recorded tenants in our study area. Interestingly, the relationship is so systematic that it unambiguously suggests that the predominantly tenant-operated households are the ones with a lower availability of owned cultivated area in relation to farm workers available in their families. (Conversely, these are the households endowed with a greater availability of farm family workers in relation to owned cultivated area.) In

[19] This is actually an index obtained by dividing the sum of area leased in during Kharif and Rabi/Boro seasons by the sum of operated area for the two seasons.

Table 4.10
Extent of Tenancy and Farm Family Resources: Two Regions Combined

Proportion of leased-in area to operated area	No. of households	Per family worker		
		Owned cultivated area (in acre)	*Value of draught animals (Rs.)*	*Value of implements and machinery (Rs.)*
A. UNRECORDED TENANTS				
Less than 0.20	37	0.61	470.70	508.35
0.20–0.39	27	0.38	382.78	657.72
0.40–0.59	21	0.18	228.12	334.04
0.60–0.79	12	0.10	234.05	120.06
0.80 & above	24	0.01	264.10	71.96
Overall	121	0.31	342.20	386.93
B. RECORDED TENANTS				
Less than 0.20	27	0.63	497.20	348.76
0.20–0.39	20	0.33	341.48	395.60
0.40–0.59	14	0.24	293.28	97.76
0.60–0.79	13	0.09	203.21	72.17
0.80 & above	29	0.05	211.69	46.00
Overall	103	0.29	321.75	182.73

their case, the need to supplement land is indeed quite acute. The assured and adequate availability of family farm labour facilitates this process more readily than in other cases.

Among the other prospective determinants of the extent of leasing-in land, Table 4.10 seems to suggest a negative association between the proportion of leased in area and the value of draught animals per worker or the value of implements and machinery per worker. However, in all these cases, the relationship is not as systematic or neat as we have observed for owned land per worker.

To the extent that predominantly tenant-operated households (for whom the proportion of leased-in area is higher) in our study areas are the ones with lower per worker values of capital resources such as draught power and farm machinery, our data do not reveal greater availability of these factors as a necessary pre-condition for entering the land-lease market by the households. On the other hand, the greater availability of farm workers in the family in relation to owned land under cultivation (that is, lower land-labour ratio) alone turns out to be the most important determinant. To put it differently, in an area characterized by very low land-labour ratio and inadequately formed labour market, the household's desire for augmenting area under cultivation so as to better utilize its surplus labour resources acts as an important motivating force for entering into tenancy arrangement. As a matter of fact, so big is the pressure to augment land area that even slightly more exploitative terms of tenancy may not deter small/petty tillers to enter the land-lease market. The availability of family farm labour in such a situation tends not only to facilitate the process of cultivating extended land area but also neutralizes some of the negative aspects of terms of tenancy. After all, every accrual of additional farm output is a net gain to them.

The foregoing discussion has an obvious limitation in that it does not explain the difference among the tenant households in terms of absolute area leased in. Consequently, while using the procedure described for classification of the tenant households, a household having no land or a negligible area of its own would turn out to be purely/predominantly tenant household even if it actually leases in a small piece of land. On the other hand, the person falling in the higher ownership size-group of landholding need not be designated as such even when he has leased-in substantial amount of area. Clearly, the index comprising the ratio of leased-in area to operated area (used a little while before) vitiates the actual differences among the households in terms of absolute area leased in.

In order to provide more rigour to the test of the impact of farm resource endowment on the extent of tenancy, we carry our discussion further to examine if absolute area leased in by the households can also be related to some of their resource endowment variables. Thus, we again distribute the households into various groups depending upon the extent of area leased in (in acres). Our main objective here is to examine whether there exists some association between acreage under tenancy and endowment of farm resources. The variables representing resource endowments are: (*a*) owned area (in acres); (*b*) number of farm family workers; (*c*) value of draught animals (Rs.); and (*d*) value of implements and machinery (Rs.).

Table 4.11 provides information on the distribution of the unrecorded and the recorded tenants into various groups depending

Table 4.11

Acreage Under Tenancy and Farm Family Resources: Two Regions Combined

Area leased in (acres)	No. of house-holds	Per household value of			
		Owned area (acres)	Farm family workers (no.)	Draught animals (Rs.)	Implements & machinery (Rs.)
A. UNRECORDED TENANTS					
Less than 0.50	38	1.48	3.26	914.47	912.21
0.50–0.99	28	1.31	3.21	974.99	914.11
1.00–1.49	22	1.32	3.27	1004.55	1006.13
1.50–2.49	25	1.18	4.12	1481.99	1769.40
2.50 & above	8	1.83	5.00	3100.00	4093.50
B. RECORDED TENANTS					
Less than 0.50	30	1.63	3.17	990.00	444.33
0.50–0.99	25	0.76	3.12	552.00	491.44
1.00–1.49	17	1.35	.4.00	1517.64	1427.23
1.50–2.49	19	1.56	4.00	1636.84	814.27
2.50 & above	12	1.23	5.25	1733.33	387.67

upon their acreage under tenancy. It clearly emerges from the table that both the unrecorded and the recorded tenants with a higher availability of farm family workers tend to lease in a greater area. A similar (positive) relationship is also discernible between acreage under tenancy and per farm values of draught animals and farm machinery in the case of unrecorded tenants. As regards the recorded tenants, however, such a relationship does not appear to be very clear and systematic.

The two sets of results obtained by relating the extent of tenancy (defined in two different ways) need not be confused as they explain two different aspects of the story. The first set clearly pin-points the fact that predominantly tenant-operated households (not necessarily the ones with larger absolute area under tenancy) have a lower availability of owned cultivated area in relation to farm family workers and this provides the greatest motivational force for them to enter into tenancy arrangements. This only reveals the compulsion exerted on a section of land-constrained tenants to enter the land-lease market in the event of a lack of alternative employment opportunities for their family resources (mostly labour).

How many of the tenant households are actually successful in attracting larger area under tenancy (in absolute term) and whether this is determined by their resource endowments are the questions explained by the second set of our analysis. Interestingly, even in this case, availability of farm family workers turned out to be the important determinant in most of the cases. This, in conjunction with the foregoing discussion, leads us to the conclusion that while greater availability of farm family labour in general motivates a section of peasants to enter into tenancy arrangements, it also facilitates to attract a larger absolute area under tenancy. On this count, tenancy in our study regions may be viewed as a means for better utilization of labour resources as well as equalizing land-labour ratio across the rural households.[20]

Choice of contractual form: We have discussed in general terms the motivations for leasing in land by the households in our study area. What determines the choice of a particular contract is, however, not clear from the preceding analysis. This becomes an important question in a situation where some tenants involve themselves in crop-sharing arrangements while others prefer fixed-rent tenancy. Such differences in contractual form even within a region have been explained by the scholars in various ways.[21] One of the explanations has been in terms of differences in 'entreprenurial ability' of the tenant households. The main argument has been that the households with higher 'entreprenurial ability' would opt for fixed-rent contracts so as to make fuller utilization of their skill and then maximize entrepreneurial profit. What is, however, lacking in such a construction of tenant behaviour is that it leaves the choice of contractual form entirely on the tenant. This is unlikely to be the case in a region with a very low land-man ratio and where a large number of prospective tenants compete in the land-lease market. In fact what is more likely in such a situation is

[20] It is to be noted that our observation in this context is somewhat nearer to that of Pant (1983, p. 37) who studied association between family resource endowment and tenancy in some semi-arid tropical villages of Andhra Pradesh and Maharashtra. It is, however, interesting to note that using the same data set as used by Pant, Jodha (1981, pp. A125–A127) had earlier arrived at a somewhat different conclusion that tenancy in that area is primarily an out-growth of bullock power adjustment and credit market imperfections rather than a mechanism of equalising land-labour ratio among the rural households. Clearly, our experience does not tally with this latter view.

[21] See Chapter 1.

that the landlords would exercise their control not only in the matter of choosing the type of tenant and the form of contract but may even dictate other terms and conditions, wherever possible. In so far as the landlords enjoy some kind of monopolistic power in the land-lease market, there may be a tendency on their part to look for 'better ability' tenants on a crop-sharing basis and then reap the benefits of their better skill and effort. To the extent that the entrepreneurial ability of a household is largely governed by the endowment of his farm resources (labour and non-labour), it would not be surprising in that situation to find the tenants with better endowment of farm resources being engaged by the landlords in crop-sharing while those lacking in terms of resources being preferred as fixed-rent tenants. This latter case may also be interpreted as a device for ensuring a minimum but fixed amount of rental earning by the landlords when leased out to 'lower ability' tenants.

The foregoing hypothesis cannot be tested meaningfully in regions such as ours, which are dominated by crop-sharing tenancy. Nevertheless, with whatever data we have, some tentative analysis can be attempted to see if there exists any relationship between entreprenurial ability of tenants (reflected by their resource endowments) and the form of tenancy.[22] In this context, we examine the distribution of tenants according to the proportion of leased in area under fixed rent contract to total area loased in along with the values of the four variables representing their resource endowments (as used in Table 4.11). The relevant data are presented in Table 4.12. In keeping with our previous discussion on types of tenancy, there are very few tenants who lease in purely/predominantly on fixed-rent basis. Table 4.12 reveals that for both categories of tenants (unrecorded and recorded), there is no clear-cut and systematic relationship between the form of tenancy and the per farm availability of family workers. The same is true of other variables, such as per farm values of draught animals and farm machinery. Thus, the overall picture seems to indicate no clear relationship between the form of tenancy and the availability of farm family resources.

However, a somewhat different impression is formed if we confine our comparison between purely sharecropped (value 0.00 in col.1, Table 4.12) and purely fixed-rented holdings (value 1.00

---

[22] We have confined this discussion to the agriculturally progressive Region I only because of insignificance of fixed-rent tenancy in the backward Region II.

Table 4.12

Forms of Tenancy and Farm Family Resources

Proportion of fixed-rent area to total leased-in area	*No. of households*	*Per household value of*			
		Owned area (in acre)	*Farm family workers (No.)*	*Draught animals (Rs.)*	*Implements and machinery (Rs.)*
A. UNRECORDED TENANTS					
0.00	38	1.71	3.68	1421.05	1974.89
0.01–0.49	11	1.16	4.00	1800.00	1020.09
0.50–0.99	6	2.15	3.00	2100.00	582.83
1.00	9	1.47	2.56	1155.56	1225.67
B. RECORDED TENANTS					
0.00	40	1.81	3.93	1540.00	939.23
0.01–0.49	5	0.79	3.80	1500.00	291.80
0.50–0.99	3	1.56	5.33	666.67	408.67
1.00	8	1.26	3.88	1200.00	441.63

in col.1). It will be evident from the table that for all types of tenants (unrecorded and recorded), purely sharecropped holdings report a much higher value of all the variables representing their resource endowments compared with purely fixed-rented holdings. This lends only partial support to our hypothesis that in a rural economy characterized by very low land-man ratio and excessive demand for land under tenancy terms, the landowners, in their attempt to maximize rental earning, may enter into sharecropping contract with the tenants with larger families and a better endowment of other resources. To reiterate, our hypothesis about the 'entreprenurial ability' of the prospective lessees is tested with less than adequate data, and the conclusion about the lessor's choice in favour of 'lessees with better ability' may not be taken as final.

Differentiation within Tenantry

One view of the differentiation within the class of tenantry can be obtained from the preceding discussion on the size-class distribution of ownership/operational holdings. However, the method of classification of rural households according to landholding (ownership/operational) has recently been criticized in the literature. The main argument has been that in a situation undergoing technical change and/or tenancy reform, even a section of the well-off peasants may take on the role of lessees. Further, in order to run the process of production, these lessees are likely to depend more on the exploitation of others' labour. At the other extreme, there may exist a class of households, drawn largely from the class of poor peasants and agricultural labourers whose main source of livelihood is the sale of their labour power, but who are occasionally compelled to cultivate leased-in land as a supplementary means of subsistence. There will then be a qualitative difference in the structure of production even between the two types of lessees, primarily because of their differential production objectives: while the former thrives on the exploitation of others' labour in order to maximize profit from cultivation, the latter depends more on 'self-exploitation' on tenanted land as well as on hiring out labour in order to ensure subsistence for the family. This is the view closer to the one put forward by Patnaik. Under this situation, what is suggested is to employ the so-called 'labour-exploitation criterion' as a method of identification of agrarian classes (see Patnaik, 1987: Ch. 1).

There have, however, been strong objections against the labour-exploitation based criterion of identifying agrarian classes.[23] Since it is outside the purview of the present study to attempt a full-length discussion of the appropriateness of methods of differentiation of rural classes, we will apply a somewhat simplified version of Patnaik's criterion so as to obtain a first-hand idea about differentiation within the class of tenantry in our study area. Needless to say, such a procedure may not be adequate to capture all the differences among the tenant households. Our exercise will only differentiate between them on the basis of one principle, namely the mode of labour utilization/exploitation.

The simplified formula employed by us to demarcate various agrarian classes within the tenantry is as follows:

$$e = \frac{H_i - H_o}{F}$$

[23] See Rudra (1988: 483–500); Athreya *et al.* (1987: 147–90).

Where H_i represents labour services hired-in (in man-days) in crop production over the year; H_o denotes labour-days hired out over the year; and F stands for family labour days contributed in crop production on self-cultivated and leased-in land put together. In actuality, one can visualize a whole continuum of tenants depending upon the value of 'e'. However, for the sake of brevity, we consider the following broad categories:

Case A: e > 1. This is the case where the tenant is primarily an exploiter of others' labour, so that net labour hired-in ($H_i - H_o$) is positive and greater than the labour contributed in crop production by his own family (F). We may call such a tenant a 'rich' tenant.

Case B: $-1 \leq e \leq 1$. In this case the tenant is primarily self-employed. Although net labour hired-in can be positive or negative for the tenant, this is less than the labour put in by his family for crop production [$|H_i - H_o| < F$]. We call this a 'middle' tenant.

Case C: e < -1. This is the case where the tenant applies some labour on his owned and/or tenanted land but he works more for others than for himself [$|H_i - H_o| < O$ and $|H_i - H_o| > F$]. We may call such a tenant a 'poor' tenant.

Applying the foregoing criterion, we may examine the distribution of tenants into these categories in our study area. The relevant information is given in Table 4.13. The important points to note from the table are: First, our survey area is very well dominated by the 'middle' category of tenants. As many as 69 per cent of the unrecorded tenants and 56 per cent of the recorded tenants belong to 'middle' category and are thus primarily self-employed. Second, the percentage of 'middle' among the unrecorded tenants is slightly higher than among the recorded ones. Third, the percentage of 'poor' tenants is not very high in our study area. Between the two types of tenants, the percentage of the poor seems to be higher in the case of recorded tenants. Fourth, although the percentage of the 'rich' among the tenants has been higher than the 'poor', not a very high percentage of all tenants could be demarcated as 'rich' in our study area. As is evident from the table, nearly 21 per cent

Table 4.13
Distribution of Tenants into Different Agrarian Classes: Two Regions Combined

Class	Unrecorded tenants	Recorded tenants	All tenants
Poor	9.92 (12)	17.48 (18)	13.84 (31)
Middle	69.42 (84)	56.31 (58)	62.95 (141)
Rich	20.66 (25)	26.21 (27)	23.21 (52)

Note: Figures in parentheses indicate the number of tenants.

of the unrecorded tenants and 26 per cent of the recorded tenants could be classified as 'rich' in terms of the above criterion.

The foregoing observations imply that there are some enterprising tenants in our study area who possibly lease in land to practise cultivation on a commercial basis with the help of hired labour. The existence of 'poor' tenants side by side reveals that some of the primarily agricultural labour households also enter into the land-lease market whenever such an opportunity is available to them. In fact, in our study area, these are the tenants many of whom lease in only during the Boro season as a part of interlinked land-lease and labour contract. The majority of tenants who fall in the 'middle' category not only rely more on their family labour to run agricultural operations but in all likelihood lease in land to utilize their labour and other resources better. This lends further support to our earlier contention that in an area characterized by a low land-man ratio and lack of alternative employment opportunities, the households with greater endowment of family resources, especially labour, are likely to look for some opening in the land-lease market. This, in turn, provides an explanation of preponderance of the 'middle' category among the tenant households.

Purchase and Sale of Land by Tenant Households

In this section, we focus attention on the purchase and sale of land by the tenant households. In particular, our objective here is to see whether the tenant households also enter the land market as sellers/purchasers of land and, if they do so, what is the background of ultimate gainers/losers from the process of land transfer. For this purpose, we analyse the data, collected through our field survey, about the purchase and sale of land by the tenant households over the decade 1976–77 to 1986–87.

We divide our sample households into three categories: growing, stable and declining. The growing households are those for whom net purchase of land (defined as total area purchased minus total area sold during 1976–77 to 1986–87) is positive; for the declining households net purchase of land is negative; and the stable households either did not participate in any form of land transaction during this decade or area purchased cancelled out with area sold.[24]

Table 4.14 presents the distribution of tenant households as per the classification above. It is observed that a fairly high percentage of tenant households turn out to be 'stable'. As evident from the

Table 4.14
Distribution of Growing, Stable and Declining Households: Two Regions Combined

Household type	Unrecorded tenants	Recorded tenants	All tenants
Growing	38 (31.40)	35 (33.98)	73 (32.59)
Stable	68 (56.20)	54 (52.43)	122 (54.46)
Declining	15 (12.40)	14 (13.59)	29 (12.95)

Note: Figures in the parentheses are percentages to total households.

table, nearly 54 per cent of all tenants fall in this category. There is not much difference in the percentage of 'stable' households between the recorded and the unrecorded tenants. Another interesting point that emerges from Table 4.14 is that quite a substantial percentage of tenant households in both the regions have gained in terms of net purchase of land over the last ten years. Nearly 31 per cent of the unrecorded tenants and 34 per cent of the recorded tenants are thus included in the category of 'growing' households. Yet another striking conclusion is that the percentage of 'declining' households among the tenants has not been very high in our study area. In fact, it ranges between 12–13 per cent for all types of tenants. The picture obtained by us reveals not only the tendency among a large section of tenant households to hang on to whatever owned land

[24] In our study, we have considered transactions in cultivable land only in order to consider households' status in the land market.

they possess[25] but it also reflects a desperate attempt by some of them to add to their tiny holdings, whenever possible.

We can now look into the question of who are the gainers/losers in terms of purchase/sale of land. More specifically, which ownership size group they belong to? For this purpose, we consider ownership size group-wise distribution of growing and declining households for 1976–77 and 1986–87.[26] The relevant data on the distribution of 'growing' and 'declining' households according to size groups of their ownership holdings for the two periods are provided in Tables 4.15 and 4.16 respectively. It is evident that the number of 'growing'/'declining' households (as we have defined them) is much higher than the number of those who are actually shifted from one group to another through such transfer of land. Thus among the 73 'growing' tenant households (unrecorded and recorded put together), only 11 could improve their ownership status by moving to higher ownership size groups (Table 4.15) while only 5 out of 29 'declining' households are pushed to lower size groups through negative transfer of land (Table 4.16). This means that the quantum of land transfer has not been very sizeable over the past decade, and could not, therefore, bring about drastic changes in ownership status even for households so affected.[27]

Another interesting aspect of the transfer of land in our study area is that the 'growing' tenant households which moved to higher ownership categories through the purchase of land mostly belonged to the lowest ownership category (less than 1.00 acre) in 1976–77 (Table 4.15). On the other hand, the 'declining' households who suffered the greatest jolt in terms of sale of land seem to belong to relatively higher categories (Table 4.16). This indicates that land market transactions have an in-built tendency towards equalization of landholdings.[28] However, if we go by the number of 'growing/

[25] This provides an indirect support to the *'stabilisation* of the small peasantry' hypothesis advanced recently by Bhaduri *et al.* (1986). Italics added.

[26] The households are divided into four size groups of ownership holdings: (*a*) less than 1.0 acre; (*b*) 1.0–2.49 acres; (*c*) 2.50–4.99 acres; and (*d*) 5.00 acres and above.

[27] This leads us to a situation similar to what has been observed by Rao (1972: A143) in Ryotwari areas of Maharashtra and Gujarat and by Bliss and Stern (1982: 45) in village Palanpur (Uttar Pradesh) as regards purchase and sale of land. Both of these studies observe a general tendency on the part of the rural communities to adhere to whatever land they possess.

[28] Although the total effect of equalization is only marginal.

Table 4.15
Distribution of Growing Households by Size-Group of Ownership Holdings (number)

Tenant type	Year	Ownership size-groups (in acres)				
		Less than 1.00	1.00 to 2.49	2.50 to 4.99	5.00 and above	Total
Unrecorded	1986–87	9	19	8	2	38
	1976–77	19	12	5	2	38
	Net change	−10	7	3	0	0
Recorded	1986–87	11	12	9	3	35
	1976–77	12	16	6	1	35
	Net change	−1	−4	3	2	0
All	1986–87	20	31	17	5	73
	1976–77	31	28	11	3	73
	Net change	−11	3	6	2	0

Table 4.16
Distribution of Declining Households by Size-Group of Ownership Holdings (number)

Tenant type	Year	Ownership size-groups (in acres)				
		Less than 1.00	1.00 to 2.49	2.50 to 4.99	5.00 and above	Total
Unrecorded	1986–87	6	6	1	2	15
	1976–77	4	6	3	2	15
	Net change	2	0	−2	0	0
Recorded	1986–87	8	4	2	0	14
	1976–77	5	6	2	1	14
	Net change	3	−2	0	−1	0
All	1986–87	14	10	3	2	29
	1976–77	9	12	5	3	29
	Net change	5	−2	−2	−1	0

declining' households falling under various size groups of ownership holdings, it appears that a majority of them belong to lower ownership size groups. What motivates a section of these lower categories of households to purchase/sell a part of their holdings is an important question which requires further probing.

In Table 4.17, we report the reasons provided by the 'declining' households behind sale of their land. It is observed that the primary reason for sale of land is to fulfil their social obligations (mostly daughter/sister's marriage). There are few instances where tenants sold land for consumption/medical needs or to repay old debt. All these reflect distress conditions of these tenants forcing them to part with their land. It may be emphasized that such households were very few in our sample.

Table 4.17
Reason for Selling Land by the Tenant Households

Reasons	Unrecorded tenants	Recorded tenants	All tenants
Consumption plus medical	–	3	3
Social purposes	16	10	26
Loan repayment	1	2	3
Purchase of draught cattle	1	–	1
Others	2	2	4
Total number of sales	20	17	37

We have also enquired from the 'growing' households as to what motivates them to acquire more land in preference to non-land assets. As evident from Table 4.18, in an overwhelming majority of the cases, the reason put forward is 'to augment owned area under cultivation'. Thus, out of 54 cases of land purchase by the unrecorded tenants, in 42 cases, the desire for augmenting owned area motivated thém to acquire more land through purchases. In the case of recorded tenants, in 40 out of 49 cases this was the reason. There are some instances where the tenants took over through purchases the ownership of previously tenanted land. However, the incidence of such type of transfer has not been very high. The overall situation seems to suggest that constrained by limited land base of their own, some households not only enter into tenancy arrangement but also try to augment their land base through purchases whenever they can afford to and their preference for land in lieu of non-land assets indicates an acute state of land hunger among them.

One may also like to know who are the buyers of land sold by the 'declining' households. As evident from Table 4.19, in our study area, a majority of such purchasers belong to the class of cultivators. Although there were a few cases of land being trans-ferred to primarily non-cultivating interests (such as businessmen,

Table 4.18

Reason for Purchase of Land by the Tenant Households

Reasons	Unrecorded tenants	Recorded tenants	All tenants
To augment owned area under cultivation	42	40	82
Adjacent to owned plot	3	–	3
Belonged to near relation	3	2	5
Previously under tenancy contract	5	7	12
Others	1	–	1
Total number of purchases	54	49	103

Table 4.19

Economic Status of Buyers of Land Sold by the Tenant Households

Reasons	Unrecorded tenants	Recorded tenants	All tenants
Cultivator	15	11	26
Serviceman	1	2	3
Businessman/Trader	2	4	6
Goldsmith	2	–	2
Others	–	–	–
Total cases	20	17	37

traders and servicemen), by and large, it has been a transfer from one section of cultivators to another. An almost similar impression can be gathered by an examination of the background of the sellers of land purchased by the 'growing' tenant households. As is clear from Table 4.20, a majority of sellers of land to the 'growing' households have themselves been cultivators. There are also some instances of non-cultivating people reducing their landed interest. This is possibly a gradually developing phenomenon under the changed circumstances in rural Bengal where non-cultivating land-owners are under tremendous pressure; thanks to vigorous application of tenancy reform measures as well as enforcement of minimum wage laws for agricultural labourers which render adoption of indirect methods of cultivation through hired labour or leasing arrangement difficult.

Table 4.20
Economic Status of Sellers of Land Bought by the Tenant Households

Reasons	Unrecorded tenants	Recorded tenants	All tenants
Cultivator	38	30	68
Serviceman	9	4	13
Businessman/Trader	6	9	15
Goldsmith	–	–	–
Others	1	6	7
Total cases	54	49	103

Our survey data show that the category comprising owner-cum-tenants predominates the land-lease market and there are very few pure tenants in our study area.

The recorded and unrecorded tenants do not differ much in terms of their economic status (as revealed by their landholding position). However, in terms of social background (indicated by caste distribution and educational level), the unrecorded tenants seem to occupy a superior position. Further, the recorded tenants belong more to the traditional sharecropper-cum-agricultural labour families as opposed to the case with the unrecorded tenants who are relatively new entrants in the land-lease market.

Our analysis on the ownership size group-wise distribution of the lessors specific to each group of lessee reveals a tendency of smaller unrecorded lessees leasing in from smaller lessors while bigger unrecorded lessees being preferred by bigger lessors. The situation is, however, different in the case of the lessors specific to the recorded lessees. All categories of recorded lessees have in general leased-in more from lessors of higher categories and no clear relationship seems to exist between the cultivating status of the recorded lessees and the ownership status of their lessors.

The distribution of lease units by lessee-lessor groups indicates that there exists no tie-up between the lessee to a specific lessor. Between the two types of lessees, the unrecorded ones have been able to attract greater number of lessors and the lessors also place them high in order of preference owing to their greater 'trustworthiness'.

As regards the differences in socio-economic status between the lessors and the lessees (both recorded and unrecorded), the former appear to display a superior position. Another important point to note is that a majority of the lessors of the unrecorded lessees have self-cultivation as the main occupation. In the case of the recorded lessees, a majority of their lessors seem to be engaged in non-agricultural activities.

Our discussion on the incidence of leasing-in land by the tenants reveals that the land-lease market works more flexibly during the Boro/Rabi season and the unrecorded tenants of lower size groups obtain precedence in the case of such seasonal tenancy arrangements. Sharecropping has been the dominant form of tenancy during the Kharif season. However, a tendency is discernible among the unrecorded tenants of lower farm size categories to lease in more land during the Boro/Rabi season under fixed produce contract. A crop-wise break-up of the lease contracts further reveals that the predominance of sharecropping has been almost exclusive in case of the traditional crop such as Aman paddy. However, with the progress of agriculture and the emergence of new crops, such as Boro paddy, tenancy has been changing its form, albeit at a slower rate, by giving way to fixed rent arrangement.

Analysing the relationship between extent of tenancy and endowment of resources among the tenant families, we discover that greater availability of farm family workers in relation to owned land under cultivation motivates a large section of poor (near-landless) peasants to enter into tenancy contracts. Thus, tenancy acts as a mechanism of equalizing labour-land ratio among the rural households.

Differentiation of tenants on the basis of mode of labour utilization/exploitation shows preponderance of the 'middle' category in our survey area. These are the tenants who depend mostly on their family labour to run agricultural operations. In an area characterized by low land-man ratio and lack of alternative employment of their available resources, these households always try to enter into tenancy arrangement which in turn explain their preponderance in the land-lease market.

The discussion on the purchase/sale of land by the tenant households reveals a tendency on their part to stick on to whatever land they possess. However, there are some instances (though not many in our study area) of households being forced to part with their holdings under the compulsion of social obligations and/or distress conditions. There are also some, albiet very few, instances of tenants augmenting their land base through purchases. Our inquiry into the question of what makes some of the tenant households to acquire additional land in preference to other non-land assets reveals that, constrained by limited land base, these households not only opt for obtaining land on tenancy terms but also seek to augment their land base through purchases as and when such an opportunity is created for them. However, thanks to their limited earning opportunities, this latter option does not seem to be available to a large section of households. Consequently, tenancy is likely to continue as a very important means of augmenting area under cultivation by them.

5

Tenancy Contracts in Actual Operation: Terms and Conditions

The main purpose of this chapter is to discuss the terms and conditions of tenancy contracts with the help of our field data collected from twelve villages in district Midnapore of West Bengal. We argued at the outset of the previous chapter that the actual terms and conditions of tenancy may be determined by the relative bargaining power of the lessors and lessees but the bargaining power cannot always be indexed merely in terms of socio-economic status of one party vis-à-vis the other or in terms of its share in the distribution of land and other farm assets. This is more so in a region which is undergoing considerable political mobilization and organization of the tenantry and other poorer sections in the rural society. This means that the tenants, although endowed with an inferior socio-economic status, may yet succeed in altering the old character of tenancy in their favour. This they can do by acquiring organizational strength (which, in turn, raises their bargaining power) thanks to their political mobilization and thanks also to the support rendered by government through various policies and programmes. More expressly, in the context of West Bengal, mobilization of a large section of tenants has indeed taken place in recent years and the government too responded seriously to serve the economic interests of this most underprivileged section of the rural society.[1] To what extent the tenants have been able, under the changed circumstances, to destroy the old tenurial relations

[1] This is clear from our discussion in Chapter 3 above. It is not only that the programme of Operation Barga was undertaken with the utmost sincerity in order to record the names of the sharecroppers so as to entitle them legal protection against rent-enhancement and eviction; several other programmes such as credit support to the recorded sharecroppers have been initiated in recent years.

and reset the terms and conditions of tenancy in their favour are important questions to which not much attention has yet been spared by researchers.[2] We thus discuss here the issue of changing terms and conditions of tenancy in the aftermath of their organized struggle through a programme such as Operation Barga (O.B.). In order to bring more clearly into focus the impact of such a movement on tenurial relations, we would specifically concentrate on the tenancy arrangements prevailing between the unrecorded tenants and the recorded tenants (i.e., the participants in O.B. programme) and their landlords in our sample area. This would enable empirical testing of the hypothesis that as the tenants start enjoying collective and organized strength, the old tenancy relations which characterize their exploitation start breaking up.

In our examination of terms and conditions of tenancy contracts, we would specifically concentrate on such aspects as crop-sharing, cost-sharing, interlinking of tenancy with other factor markets and a few other conditions governing the tenancy contracts.

Crop-sharing Patterns

Crop-sharing tenancy has its own variants which need not be spelt out here. Nevertheless, it is highly instructive to examine the variants which are emerging between the unrecorded and the recorded tenants and their respective landlords in our study area. Before we do so, it is worthwhile to recall that other researchers have noted a wide variety of crop-sharing patterns for the state of West Bengal. For example, using data for 110 villages in the state, Bardhan and Rudra (1980: 294) observed as many as eleven different types of crop-shares prevailing in 1975–76.[3] In recent years, the number of crop-share variants has tended to decline. Thus, in the 1979–80 study conducted by Khasnabis and Chakraborty (1982: A24) in the Nadia district of West Bengal, only four types of crop-shares have been highlighted. In another study by Chattopadhyay

[2] Our discussion in the concluding section of Chapter 3 shows that even the assessment by the so-called serious critics of the O.B. programme is based on conjecture rather than the examination of the empirical reality of changing tenurial relations consequent upon the adoption of this programme.

[3] In an earlier study covering eighty-one villages spread over the whole state, Rudra (1975: A59) also observed a similar pattern.

and Ghosh (1983: A75) in 1981–82 in the 'terai' area of Darjeeling district, crop-sharing was reported only in three different forms. It is, however, not very clear from these studies if the observed reduction in the number of share-crop variants is due to a large section of the tenants being able to exercise their tenurial rights in recent years. Nor can it be authenticated from these studies if the pattern of crop-sharing for different crops has responded to differences in the levels of technology available for individual crops.

We present our data on crop-sharing patterns separately for individual crops and for the two groups of tenants. As is evident from Table 5.1, a maximum of five different crop-sharing patterns are conceivable for our study area for the two most important crops Aman paddy and Boro (summer) paddy.[4] Our data clearly indicate a persistent tendency for the crop-sharing arrangement to hover around 50:50 division of produce for the former crop, particularly in the case of the unrecorded tenants. Thus in 75 of a total of 80 cases (nearly 94 per cent), equal sharing of Aman paddy took place between the unrecorded tenants and their landlords. Although the observed variation in crop-sharing is higher in the case of recorded tenants, there is a clear tendency towards a large section of them retaining more than 50 per cent of the crop. As is clear from Table 5.1, the recorded tenants' share in Aman paddy has been more than 50 per cent in 60 out of 80 cases (75 per cent). It is, however, striking that in one-fourth of the cases, these tenants maintain their traditional arrangement of equal sharing in case of Aman paddy even though recording of their tenanted plots entitle them to three-fourths of the gross produce if the landlords have not participated in the cost of cultivation.[5]

The crop-sharing pattern for Boro paddy is different from that in Aman paddy. For this crop, the predominant pattern is the one where 75 per cent of the crop is retained by the tenant. Thus in 73 out of a total of 96 cases (nearly 76 per cent), the unrecorded

---

[4] We have not attempted any separate discussion on sharing patterns for the main crop as well as the by-product. This is because in most of the cases in our study area, sharing took place before threshing and hence sharing of by-product followed the sharing of main crop. However, in cases where the tenant performed threshing, the entire by-product accrued to him.

[5] Such a situation need not be interpreted as the tenants' failure to exercise their crop-sharing rights as stipulated in the Act even after recording. On the contrary, it has been divulged by many such tenants that they themselves voluntarily offered equal share of crop so as to maintain good relations with their landlords.

Table 5.1
Frequency Distribution of Crop Shares (Number of Cases)

Crop	Tenant type	Crop share (Tenant: Owner)					Total cases
		1:0 (100%)	3:1 (75%)	2:1 (67%)	3:2 (60%)	1:1 (50%)	
Aman paddy	UR	1	1	–	3	75	80
	R	25	30	4	1	20	80
Boro paddy	UR	–	73	1	2	20	96
	R	21	31	–	–	4	56
Aus paddy	UR	1	–	–	–	1	2
	R	1	1	–	–	3	5
Jute	UR	1	4	–	7	14	26
	R	1	5	3	–	2	11
Potato	UR	–	23	–	1	–	24
	R	–	1	–	–	–	1
Sugarcane	UR	–	–	–	–	3	3
	R	4	5	–	–	3	12

Note: UR = Unrecorded; R = Recorded.

tenants obtained three-fourths share of the gross produce. The pattern of crop-sharing for Boro paddy suggests a different picture under the improved technological conditions. With the utilization of purchased inputs such as high-yielding seeds, chemical fertilizers, insecticides and pesticides, irrigation, and so on tending to become a normal practice with most cultivators, a large section of tenants find it highly uneconomical to part with more than 25 per cent or so of produce for this crop. This tendency has been more prominent among the recorded tenants.

Table 5.1 also reveals the pattern of crop-sharing for some other crops. As regards jute, there is equal-sharing in a good number of cases by the unrecorded tenants while the recorded tenants tended to retain more than 50 per cent of output as their share. A similar trend is noticeable in the case of another commercial crop, sugarcane. However, in the case of potato, both types of tenants received three-fourths of the crop. For another traditional crop (i.e., Aus paddy), equal-sharing predominates for both types of tenants.

The overall pattern of crop-sharing in our study area suggests the predominance of equal-sharing for traditional crops (such as Aman paddy) for the unrecorded tenants. In the case of recorded tenants, however, a strong tendency seems to be emerging with them to retain more than 50 per cent of this crop as their share. In spite of some instances of this crop being equally shared between the recorded tenants and their landlords, there is imposing evidence in support of our premise that in the aftermath of the organized struggle by the tenants in West Bengal in recent years, the crop-sharing pattern has become more favourable to the tenants even for the traditional crops. In other words, it appears that the recorded tenants, although still in an extremely inferior socio-economic position vis-à-vis their landlords, are nevertheless able to exercise their legal rights in the matter of crop-sharing. On this count, our finding contradicts the position taken by some researchers that large-scale peasant mobilizations have not been successful in altering, *inter alia*, the old pattern of crop-sharing in favour of the tenants.[6] The tendency of tenants getting larger (three-fourths) share of output has been even greater in the case of Boro paddy, unmistakably in the case of the recorded tenants.

Pattern of Cost-sharing

In the theoretical literature, the phenomenon of cost-sharing has been interpreted as a means to correct distortions in the use of some inputs (e.g., fertilizer). If the tenant has insufficient incentive to use some inputs, participation in cost by the landlord may induce their optimum utilization. It is for the sake of encouraging application of variable inputs in 'socially efficient amounts' by the tenants that some scholars have suggested the principle of landlords sharing input costs in the same proportion as output (see Adams and Rask, 1968: 941). The sharecropping arrangements indeed show some kind of cost-sharing, at least in some cases.[7] However, there are several departures from the suggested rule of setting cost-share equal to output share. Under this situation, the issues which come into the forefront are: (a) under what conditions does the landlord share in cost or what is the rationale behind cost-sharing arrangements; and (b) what determines the equilibrium cost-sharing rules under sharecropping.

[6] This is the position held for example by Chattopadhyay and Ghosh (1983: A76).

[7] See, for example, Rudra (1975b); Bardhan and Rudra (1980).

These are the issues which have prompted some theoretical model-building in recent years by a band of neoclassical economists. For example, Braverman and Stiglitz (1986: 642–52) in one of their recent papers sought to answer these questions in terms of what may be called 'Imperfect Information Paradigm'. Following their argument, the landlord can monitor the application of inputs (labour and non-labour) so as to remove inefficiency of resource allocation by the tenant so long as there is symmetric information between him and the tenant concerning the production conditions. In so far as there is information asymmetry or the tenant has better knowledge concerning the optimum level of input and the changes to be undertaken in its utilization in response to changes such as those in weather and soil conditions, the landlord has to design the contract in such away that the tenant is induced to adjust his input in response to these changes. Under a situation of asymmetric information, therefore, some cost-sharing becomes inevitable at least for the sake of better utilization of some input factors. This leads them to the conclusion that 'cost-sharing contracts have a decided advantage over contracts which specify the level of inputs whenever there are asymmetries of information regarding production technology between the landlord and the tenant' (Braverman and Stiglitz, 1986: 652). As regards the other question of deviation from the simple rule of cost-sharing being equal to output-sharing, the authors argue that if the level of effort (labour) cannot be precisely foreseen and specified in the contract, then by sharing more in the cost of inputs (for instance, fertilizers) which are strongly complementary to labour, the landlord may induce greater effort by the tenant. Furthermore, sharing more in the cost of input enables the landlord to increase his output share by keeping the tenant at the same level of expected utility since it also reduces the risk that he faces. In any case, cost-sharing in the neoclassical tradition has been interpreted as a mechanism adopted by the landlord to ensure efficient application of inputs as also to augment his share of output under the presence of information asymmetry. The validity or otherwise of such a theory cannot be tested meaningfully in a region such as ours where, as will be evident from the discussion below, the incidence of cost-sharing by the landlords has been very low. However, it will not be difficult to establish in course of our discussion that whatever evidence of cost-sharing exists, is motivated by the landlords solely to extract larger share of output.

Cost-sharing in the areas of our study takes place mostly in respect of fertilizer input and in some specific instances, for insecticides and pesticides and for irrigation. The cost of all other inputs is the responsibility of the tenant. Moreover, the pattern of cost-sharing has not been uniform for all crops as also between the landlords of the unrecorded and the recorded tenants. As is evident from Table 5.2, cost-sharing whenever it exists, has been a phenomenon associated with the cultivation of Boro paddy. In the case of Aman paddy, the incidence of cost-sharing by the landlords has been very low. Further, although in all of the 80 cases where the unrecorded tenants reported to have used fertilizer for the cultivation of Aman paddy, only in twelve cases the cost is shared by the landowners (either equally or fully), while in the rest of the cases, its costs is borne entirely by the tenants. As regards other inputs such as insecticides and pesticides and irrigation, their cost too is borne almost entirely by the tenants. The incidence of cost-sharing for Aman paddy by the landlords of the recorded tenants is rather negligible in our study area. Only in one out of a total of eighty cases, these tenants equally shared the cost of fertilizer alone with their landlords.

There is some, albeit *very limited*, indication that landlords of the unrecorded tenants are showing some interest in cost-participation in the case of Boro paddy. In the case of recorded tenants, almost the entire costs are their own responsibility. However, the overall picture on the pattern and extent of cost-sharing by the landlords of these two categories of tenants do not seem to be adequately clear to support generalizations made by other researchers, namely, that cost-sharing has been a striking phenomenon in respect of landlords of the unrecorded tenants or that recording of tenancy rights discourages landlords to participate in sharing of cost of cultivation.[8] On the contrary, sporadic instances of cost-sharing notwithstanding, our data tend to suggest that, in general, the incidence of cost-sharing has generally been very low among the landlords. More importantly, we do not observe very significant difference in the incidence of cost-sharing between the unrecorded and the recorded tenants. The slightly higher tendency of cost-sharing in the case of unrecorded tenants does not at all warrant the conclusion that the recorded tenants are being thrown to a

[8] This is the view most strongly expressed by Rudra (1981: A65).

Table 5.2
Frequency Distribution of Cost Shares (Number of Cases)

Crop	Tenant type	Cost share (Tenant: Owner)									Total cases
		Fertilizer			Insec. & pesticides			Irrigation			
		1:0 (100%)	1:1 (50%)	0:1 (0%)	1:0 (100%)	1:1 (50%)	0:1 (0%)	1:0 (100%)	1:1 (50%)	0:1 (0%)	
Aman paddy	UR	68	8	4	80	–	–	8	8	–	80
	R	79	1	–	80	–	–	5	–	–	80
Boro paddy	UR	83	9	4	91	5	–	92	3	1	96
	R	53	3	–	55	1	–	56	–	–	56
Jute	UR	20	6	–	26	–	–	22	4	–	26
	R	10	1	–	11	–	–	9	2	–	11
Potato	UR	24	–	–	24	–	–	24	–	–	24
	R	1	–	–	1	–	–	–	–	–	1
Sugarcane	UR	2	1	–	3	–	–	3	–	–	3
	R	11	1	–	12	12	–	–	11	1	12

Note: UR = Unrecorded; R = Recorded.

position of disadvantage in that their landlords have completely stopped the practice of cost-sharing. The moot point is that the incidence of cost-sharing is very low, whether for unrecorded or recorded tenants.

Association between crop and cost shares: In spite of the rather fragmentary nature of cost participation by landlords for both types of tenants, it may be useful to ask whether there exists any association between the patterns of crop and cost-sharing by the landlords. The relevant data concerning the possible association for the two most important crops namely Aman paddy and Boro paddy are set out in Table 5.3. It is interesting to note that no cost-sharing exists for Aman paddy for either of the tenant groups when the tenants retain more than 50 per cent of the crop as their share. Even where equal-sharing prevails for Aman paddy, landlords' participation in cost has not been very significant. Further, among the cases where unrecorded tenants equally share the crop Aman paddy, only in 28.8 per cent of the cases the landlords share at least one of the items of cost. The participation in cost among the equal crop-sharing cases for the recorded tenants has been lower in the case of Aman paddy compared with that for the unrecorded tenants. Such a low level of participation in cost even when the landowners are offered a share of the crop larger than the one stipulated by the Tenancy Act[9] could be due to the fact that the utilization of purchased inputs (fertilizer, insecticides and pesticides and irrigation) in the case of this traditional crop do not assume a level so as to necessitate immediate participation in cost by the landowners. The cultivation of Boro paddy, however, requiring larger doses of purchased inputs duly warrants landlords' participation in cost of cultivation whenever they obtain equal share of output. As is evident from Table 5.3, in 94.1 per cent of the cases where the output of Boro paddy has been equally shared between the unrecorded tenants and their landlords, the latter participated in cost of at least one input. Although the incidence of equal crop-sharing cases is not very high for Boro paddy among the recorded

[9] It may be noted that as per the prevailing Tenancy Acts in the state, the landowners are entitled to 25 per cent of gross produce on their leased-out land in the event of non-participation in cost. However, they are entitled to get 50 per cent of gross produce if they supplied all inputs other than labour (i.e. plough, cattle, manure, seeds and other inputs necessary for cultivation).

Table 5.3
Association between Cost Shares and Crop Shares (Percentage)

Crop	Unrecorded tenants: Cost-sharing			Recorded tenants: Cost-sharing		
	Exists	*Does not exist*	*Total*	*Exists*	*Does not exist*	*Total*
Aman Paddy						
Tenant's share above 50 per cent	0.0	100.0	100.0 (6.2)	0.0	100.0	100.0 (75.0)
Tenant's share & owner's share 50:50	28.8	71.2	100.0 (93.8)	5.2	94.8	100.0 (25.0)
Boro Paddy						
Tenant's share above 50 per cent	0.0	100.0	100.0 (79.2)	1.8	98.2	100.0 (92.9)
Tenant's share & owner's share 50:50	94.1	5.9	100.0 (20.8)	50.0	50.0	100.0 (7.1)

Notes: 1. The figures in the brackets are the percentages of the two groups of crop shares.
2. For finding association between cost and crop shares, the cases of fixed produce/cash contracts have not been considered.
3. If the owner shared in any of the costs in fertilizer, insecticides and pesticides and irrigation, it has been considered as the case of cost-sharing.

tenants, even in one-half of such cases cost-sharing by the landlords was discernible in our study area.

The overall pattern of association of cost and crop-sharing suggests a tendency towards landlords sharing cost only when they are rewarded with larger share of the crop. Whether or not cost-sharing by the landlords is intended towards ensuring more efficient utilization of resources by the tenants, our sample data cannot answer the same adequately. However, we have fairly strong information to indicate a tendency among some of the landlords extracting share of crop greater than that stipulated in the Tenancy Act by the mechanism of cost-sharing.[10]

Some Sidelines on Tenancy Contracts

Decision-making: As regards decision regarding crop production, it is the responsibility of the tenants. All decisions regarding the choice of crops, the use of input-mix, etc. are taken by tenants in our survey area. This is typically true both for the recorded and the unrecorded tenants (except for only one case among the unrecorded tenants). This reflects the state of independence enjoyed by them in reality.

Reason for non-recording: We have enquired into the question of why some tenants have not gone in for recording of their names and preferred to remain unrecorded. The most frequent answer has been 'to maintain long-standing good relations with the land-lord'. With 46 out of a total of 121 unrecorded tenants, this was the reason for opting against recording. The seasonal nature of tenancy arrangements has also been responsible for non-recording in a good number of cases. In 40 cases, the tenants abstained from recording as they leased in land for one season only. In 14 cases the tenants revealed their faith in mutual relation while in another 13 cases, they reported family ties with the landlord as the reason for non-recording. The overall picture seems to indicate that it has been a voluntary decision by a section of tenants not to go in for

---

[10] This can also be confirmed by the results of Chi-square test conducted to measure the association between crop-share and cost-share. The test results presented below show that association between crop and cost shares has been significant for both Aman paddy and Boro paddy as well as for both categories of tenants.

Measures of Association Between Crop and Cost Shares

Crop	Tenant type	Value of contingency Chi-square	Degree of freedom
Aman paddy	Unrecorded	55.25*	1
	Recorded	22.28*	1
Boro paddy	Unrecorded	80.06*	1
	Recorded	51.60*	1

Note: *means significant at 1 per cent level.

recording. Further, on the strength of our field data, we have no reason to believe that the semi-feudal authority, in order to deprive the tenants from legally stipulated share of produce, prevented some of them from recording their names.[11]

Relations after recording: As regards the question of changing relations between the landlord and the tenant after recording, it is observed that while recording does provide security against eviction and rent-enhancement to the tenant, it may also put under strain their previous relation. Thus, although in 42 out of a total of 103 cases, the tenants found the relations with the landlords after recording 'unchanged', in 53 cases they reported deterioration in their relationship. It is also reported that in some of these cases, the landlords often refused to accept their stipulated share of crop and every effort on the part of the tenants to restore a workable relation with them has been frustrated by the non-responsiveness of their landlords.[12]

Political affiliation: The nature of political affiliation of tenant households has also been widely commented upon in the literature on land reforms in West Bengal. We too made an inquiry in this regard. Our inquiry shows that the percentage of the members of Kisan Sabha among the recorded tenants has been much higher compared with those among the unrecorded tenants. While nearly 82 per cent of all recorded tenants reported their membership of the left-wing peasant political organization, the corresponding percentage for the unrecorded tenants was only about 45 per cent. We have thus some reason to believe that political affiliation has emboldened a very high percentage of the erstwhile unrecorded tenants to avail of the legal facility of recording.

Factor Market Interlinkages

In this section we examine the issue of interlinking of factor markets in the context of our study area. There are two contrasting views in the theoretical literature concerning interlinked rural

[11] It has been the view, to which we cannot subscribe, of Khasnabis and Chakraborty (1982: A27) that the hold of semi-feudal authority in rural areas is not allowing a large section of tenants to record their names through Operation Barga.

[12] See, in this context, Dasgupta (1987).

markets. According to one view, interlinking between land-lease and credit markets acts as a means of the exploitation of the poor tenants at the hands of the exploiter-landlord (see Bhaduri, 1973, 1983, 1986). The other view, while rejecting interlinking being necessarily exploitative, explains its rationale in terms of information asymmetry which creates a moral hazard problem and hence makes monitoring of tenant activities costly for the landlord (see Braverman and Stiglitz: 1982). Some kind of interlinking, say, between land and credit contracts, therefore, becomes necessary on consideration of improving allocative efficiency as also the welfare of the contracting parties (Mitra: 1983; Braverman and Guasch: 1984; Binswanger and Rosenzweig: 1986; Stiglitz: 1986). Both of these approaches, however, rest on an implicit assumption that there is complete dichotomization between the two classes. While the landlords, being drawn largely from big land-owning categories are rich/pure rentiers, the tenants comprising the class of the poor/landless who depend on the landlords for lease contract as well as credit support to meet their consumption and/or production needs.

Obviously, as a necessary condition, the validity of the approaches mentioned above rest on the extent of validity of rich-poor dichotomization of lessors and lessees. Under improved technological conditions with bigger cultivators also entering the land-lease market as lessees and small landowners appearing as lessors, such dichotomization fails to come true and hence the explanation for the phenomenon of interlinking on this basis gets weakened. Similarly, if in any particular region, the composition of both the lessors and the lessees be such that all come largely from lower landowning categories, the sheer inability of the former to offer credit support along with lease contract may reduce interlinking to a non-starter. Yet another possibility is the one where the lessors, despite being generally drawn from higher ownership categories, may be unwilling to offer contracts other than through land-lease market to the lessees as the latter become organized to exercise their rights which effectively reduce the control on the lessees by the lessors. In any case, it is the objective condition specific to a region which would determine the nature or even the existence of market interlinkings. In brief, there is no *a priori* ground to view interlinkages as characteristics of all epochs and all agrarian economies.

Our discussion in Chapter 2 provided some evidence of inter-linking of rural markets under colonial Bengal. The bargadars (sharecroppers) depended on their landlords for land-lease and credit contracts and they often supplied 'begar' (unpaid labour services) as part of their dependence-dominance relationship. Clearly, such a situation indeed reflects the exploitative nature of market interlinkings. In spite of continuation of dependence of sharecroppers on the landlords for many years even after Independence, only with their gradual mobilization by left political parties coupled with rigorous application of tenancy reform measures in recent years, that the tenancy relations are expected to have become more formal considerably weakening the old dependence-dominance relationship.

In Bengal today, the recorded tenants are not only in a majority but are well organized to assert their rights. To the extent that recording of land by them worsen their relationship with the landlords, one may expect under the prevailing situation that the transaction between them is confined to land-lease market only. However, the unrecorded tenants being typically involved in traditional tenancy arrangements, offer scope for their transactions with the landlords going beyond land market alone, perhaps encompassing several markets. However, even in this case, it ultimately depends on who leases from whom and one precondition for making interlinking between land-lease and credit contracts viable is that the lessors are capable of advancing loans.

The discussion in the preceding chapter provided no evidence of lessors of the unrecorded tenants being drawn unambiguously from rich/big landowning category. Rather, their lessors come from almost all size-groups, of course, with a relatively higher concentration in small and middle categories. Moreover, a substantial proportion of them report self-cultivation as the principal occupation who might have leased out temporarily owing to short-run difficulties of maintaining the process of production. As regards the class of tenants, not many of them belong to the pure tenant/landless category. In any case, the available evidence fails to provide unqualified support to the view that all lessors belong to pure rentier/rich landowning category just as all tenants are not necessarily the landless and/or poor.[13] Another important point that

---

[13] This renders most of the recently developed theoretical models on tenancy-credit interlinking inapplicable in the context of our study area.

needs to be underlined is that there is a tendency with smaller unrecorded tenants (for whom credit support is presumably more essential) getting involved into tenancy relationships with the smaller lessors while bigger lessors going in for bigger tenants. Under these circumstances, one may hypothesize a case for gradual disappearance of interlinking of land-lease and credit markets even for the unrecorded tenants.

In Table 5.4 we give information on the interlinking of land-lease and credit contracts emerging from our survey. It is rather queer that only one of the unrecorded tenants reported to have

Table 5.4

Credit taken by Tenants from Landlords (Number of Cases)

Item	Unrecorded tenants	Recorded tenants
1. Total number of tenants	121	103
2. Tenants who have taken credit during the current year for:		
(a) Consumption	–	–
(b) Production	1	–
3. (a) Tenants who approach for interest-free credit as and when required	1	–
(b) Tenants who approach for credit as and when required but pay interest at the rate charged by the *gramin mahajan*	6	1

taken production loan from his landlord during the period covered in our survey. There has also been very low incidence of tenants approaching the landlord for a loan even under extraordinary circumstances. As is evident from the table, only six out of a total of 121 unrecorded tenants revealed that they would approach their landlords for credit as and when required. In all these cases, however, they would pay interest at the rate charged by the *gramin mahajan* (village money-lender). The incidence of recorded tenants approaching landlords for credit has been almost zero. The available evidence does not support the case of tenants depending on landlords for credit; there is neither a tie-up between land-lease and credit contracts putting the tenant in an exploitative relationship vis-à-vis his landlord nor is there any indication of the latter offering credit on consideration of improving allocative efficiency of the former.[14]

There is, however, some evidence of interlinking of land-lease and labour contracts particularly in the case of unrecorded tenants. As is evident from Table 5.5, nearly a quarter of 121 unrecorded tenants lease in land as part of an interlinked land-labour contract. The incidence of tying labour through land-lease contract is,

Table 5.5
Interlinking of Tenancy and Labour Contracts (Number of Cases)

Item	Unrecorded tenants	Recorded tenants
1. Total number of tenants	121	103
2. Tenants who rendered labour services to the landlord	30	3
3. (a) Tenants who received wages at the going market rate for rendering labour services to the landlord	30	3
(b) Tenants who received wages lower than the market rate for rendering labour services to the landlord	–	–

however, insignificant in the case of recorded tenants. Among the unrecorded tenants, interlinking operates through Boro season only. Most of such tenants, being drawn largely from agricultural labour families, are offered land-lease contract with the understanding that they would offer labour services for the cultivation of self-operated land by the landlords. This cannot be interpreted as representing stereotypical feudal agrarian landlord-serf relationships as long as extra-economic coercion from the landlords is absent. Moreover, the tenants' commitment to provide labour services do

[14] It may be noted that our observation on the pattern of interlinking of land-lease and credit markets is consistent with what is observed by Khasnabis and Chakraborty (1982: A30) but it contradicts other observers on the subject such as Rudra (1975A: 1049), Bardhan and Rudra (1980: 291), and Chattopadhyay and Ghosh (1983: A77). Most of these latter studies were actually conducted in the middle or end of the seventies. It is possible that rigorous application of tenancy reform measures coupled with the spread of credit facilities in recent years have contributed to a noticeable decline in the proportion of unrecorded tenants' dependence on landowners for credit.

not forbid their right to offer them in the free labour market. During our field inquiry, it was revealed by all such tenants that they receive wages at the prevailing market rate for their services to the landlords and no effective pressure is applied on them to prevent their entry into the free labour market. In any case, the prevailing situation does not indicate feudal or semi-feudal relations of production as some scholars have forcefully opined in recent years.

Tenants' Access to Credit

Although the tenants in our study area do not depend on their landlords for a supply of credit, this does not mean that they do not require credit support. In fact, credit support is necessary, in varying degrees, for all categories of farmers in a growing agrarian economy. Just as the flow of credit fulfils the capital requirements of farmers, its non-availability or inadequate or untimely availability may pose an extremely critical obstacle to innovation. It is, therefore, necessary to examine in some detail, their position in the credit market. This would also help us to examine the validity of one of the criticisms against the recent agrarian reform policies of the Left Front Government in Bengal. The criticism is that 'barga recording' while breaking down the system of landowners making production advances to the tenants has not been followed by the opening to them of new sources of production advances.[15]

Participation in the credit market: We first examine the extent of participation in the credit market by the two categories of tenants. For this purpose, we club various sources of credit into two—institutional and non-institutional. In the former group is included credit taken from commercial banks, co-operatives and government agencies while in the latter group we include credit obtained from the *gramin mahajans*, friends and relatives, neighbours and landlords.[16]

[15] This is the view held by Rudra (1981: A65) without, however, providing any convincing empirical support in favour of his contention.

[16] It may be noted that among the sources included in the group of informal credit, the most important in our survey area is credit obtained from *gramin mahajans*.

Table 5.6 gives us interesting insights. It is evident that the percentage of households depending on institutional sources is much higher in the case of recorded tenants compared with their unrecorded brethren. The table shows that while about 44 per cent of recorded tenants depend exclusively on institutional sources of credit, the corresponding figure is only 22 per cent for the unrecorded tenants. Since a higher percentage of the recorded tenants depends on institutional credit to meet their borrowing requirements, the percentage of them depending on non-institutional sources has been naturally lower in our study area. Another point to note in this context is that the percentage of non-borrowing households has been slightly lower in the case of recorded tenants. In a broad sense, it reflects a greater urge on the part of tenants to borrow more freely after their names are duly registered.

Table 5.6
Participation in the Credit Market by Source of Credit
(percentage of borrowing households)

Item	Unrecorded tenants	Recorded tenants
Source of credit:		
(a) Institutional only	22.32	43.69
(b) Non-institutional only	25.62	14.56
(c) Both	25.62	19.42
Not borrowing	26.44	22.33
Total	100.00	100.00
	(121)	(103)

Note: Figures in the parentheses represent total number of tenants.

Amount borrowed from different sources: As regards availability of credit per borrowing household, Table 5.7 shows that a greater proportion of total credit requirement of the recorded tenants is met through the institutional agencies. Thus, while nearly 73 per cent of the total credit borrowed by recorded tenants has come from institutional sources, corresponding figure for the unrecorded tenants is 63 per cent. However, if we consider the actual amount borrowed by each borrowing household it is observed that loan amount per borrowing household is higher for the unrecorded tenant both for institutional and non-institutional loans. It is also observed that although the quantum of institutional loan received

Table 5.7

Availability of Credit per Borrowing Household by Purpose and Source (in Rupees)

Purpose	Unrecorded tenants			Recorded tenants		
	Instl.	*Non-instl.*	*Total*	*Instl.*	*Non-instl.*	*Total*
Aman cultivation	339	47	386	499	65	564
Boro cultivation	248	226	474	77	143	220
Purchase of draught cattle	449	51	500	540	8	548
Purchase of land	45	154	199	54	–	54
Consumption and health care	–	85	85	–	34	34
House construction	–	–	–	33	3	36
Social purposes	79	212	291	113	147	260
Non-agricultural uses	290	65	355	26	101	127
All purposes	1450	840	2290	1342	501	1843
	(63.3)	(36.7)	(100.0)	(72.8)	(27.2)	(100.0)

Note: Figures in parentheses indicate percentages of total.

by an unrecorded borrowing household is higher by a paltry margin of 8.0 per cent only from that for a recorded borrowing household, this margin goes up to as high as 68.0 per cent when we consider borrowings from non-institutional sources. Undoubtedly, it is clear that the unrecorded tenants are obliged to fall back upon non-institutional sources to a much bigger extent compared with their recorded counterparts.

Use of credit: It may perhaps be useful to look into the quantum of institutional and non-institutional borrowings, separately by recorded and unrecorded tenants, for different purposes. To begin with, our data (Table 5.7) clearly reveal that in respect of institutional credit obtained expressly for production purposes (credit obtained for Aman and Boro paddy cultivation and purchase of draught cattle put together), the recorded tenants are better placed. The amount received by them exceeds by 8.0 per cent over that received by the unrecorded tenants. In particular, their borrowing from institutional sources for Aman paddy cultivation is of a substantially higher magnitude. This is also true in the case of borrowing for investment in draught cattle. They receive, however, a much lower amount of institutional credit for Boro cultivation. This may partly be explained in terms of cropping pattern differences observed between the two groups of tenants. As would be evident from our discussion in the next chapter, while relatively more recorded tenants are involved in Aman cultivation, the reverse is true for Boro cultivation. Hence, their mutual differences in terms of loan requirements for Aman cultivation against Boro cultivation. Yet another striking feature of Table 5.7 is that the unrecorded tenants are getting a much higher quantum of institutional credit for non-agricultural purposes. It is possible that for some such households, the regime of uncertain stay on land is powerful enough to drive them to sundry non-agricultural activities which receive due support from official agencies under the poverty eradication programmes.

The foregoing discussion and the relative position of the recorded tenants notwithstanding, it needs to be stressed that a substantial proportion of tenant households (both recorded and unrecorded) still depend upon the non-institutional agencies to meet their credit requirements. Thus, there still remains a strong case for breaking the nexus of non-institutional lenders both in terms of covering a still larger section of recorded tenants as also supplying greater quantum of credit to each borrowing household.

Terms and conditions of borrowing non-institutional loan: In order to obtain some idea on the terms and conditions of borrowing we shall first consider the collateral offered by the households to obtain loan from the non-institutional sources. This is necessary because the type of collateral offered by the borrower determines the 'merit' of the case under which funds would be forthcoming. In so far as all households in a region do not possess similar economic status, there will be differences in the type of collateral offered by them to obtain credit from the non-institutional agencies. The households offering marketable collateral (such as land and gold) should not face much difficulty in getting loans while those lacking in this regard would obtain loans by offering anticipated labour service contracts, the sale of prospective crops, etc. The information on the collateral offered by the two categories of tenants to obtain loans from non-institutional agencies is summarized in Table 5.8. Three important points emerge in this context. First, for both categories of tenants put together, the loans from non-institutional

Table 5.8
Collaterals for Non-institutional Borrowings

Item	Unrecorded tenants	Recorded tenants	All tenants
Total number of loan contracts	69	38	107
Percentage of loan contracts with some form of collateral	81	84	82
Percentage of loan contracts with collateral as:			
Land	2	–	1
Labour	16	19	17
Product	14	28	19
Gold	68	53	63
Total	100	100	100
Percentage of loan contracts without collateral	19	16	18
Percentage of loan contracts without interest to total loan contracts	13	5	10

sources are obtained by more than 82.0 per cent of them by offering some collateral. Second, in most of the cases, the households offered gold as the collateral to obtain loans. There are also some instances of households offering labour services and standing crops as collateral. Third, between the two categories of tenants, the tendency of offering labour services/product as collateral has been higher with the recorded tenants. In most of these cases, the tenants obtained loans from the neighbours on the condition that they would repay them by providing labour services or by offering a part of their harvested crop. In a limited sense, this may perhaps be interpreted as the case of tying of credit-product or credit-labour contracts.

The terms and conditions of borrowing are also reflected by interest charged on loans. It is clear from Table 5.9 that the rate of interest charged by the non-institutional agencies was six to seven times higher than that charged by the institutional sources. For institutional loans, the average interest rate paid by the recorded tenants was lower than that paid by the unrecorded ones.[17] However, compared with the unrecorded tenants, average interest paid

---

[17] This is because a higher proportion of the recorded tenants, being lower caste/tribes, obtain institutional loans which are subsidized.

Table 5.9
Interest Rate by Type of Tenancy and Source of Lending (per cent per year)

Item	Unrecorded tenants	Recorded tenants
Institutional credit	11.61	10.24
Non-institutional credit:		
Gramin Mahajan	75.14	79.75
Neighbour	39.80	68.40
Friends & Relatives	19.50	43.50
Landlord	66.00	–
All sources	60.74	72.94

by them for non-institutional loans has been higher. Among all informal sources of credit, the rate of interest is the highest for the loans drawn from *gramin mahajans.*

It clearly emerges from our study that the recorded tenants, despite being inferior in socio-economic status, are more successful in exercising their crop-sharing rights in the aftermath of their organized struggle in the state.

The incidence of cost-sharing by landlords has been generally very low in our study area. Although the landlords of the unrecorded tenants tend to show a greater interest in cost-sharing, yet the number of such cases does not seem to be too many. It is clear enough from our analysis that practically all cases of cost-sharing seem to be motivated by the desire of the landlords to eke out larger share of the crop.

In our study area, all decisions concerning production are taken by the tenants themselves. The landlord-tenant relation worsens following the recording of land by the tenants, often leading to a flat refusal to accept the stipulated share of the crop by the landlords. As regards non-recording by a section of the tenants, the seasonal nature of lease contracts or a desire on the part of the tenants 'to maintain long-standing good relation with the landlords' appeared as important reasons. It is also possible that with a large section of the unrecorded tenants remaining outside the ambit of Kisan Sabha, they have not yet been mobilized to record their names. In any case, no imposing evidence is available in our study area to support the view that semi-feudal vested interests are preventing these tenants from going in for barga recording.

In our analysis of market interlinkings, we do not find strong evidence of interlinking between land-lease and credit contracts. Some evidence, however, is found regarding interlinking of land-lease and labour contracts, particularly in the case of the unrecorded tenants in agriculturally progressive areas. This interlinking operates mainly through the Boro season. There is, however, no indication of land-labour interlinking leading to extra-economic coercion from the landlords or the tenants losing their right to offer themselves freely in wage labour market. In the case of recorded tenants, the incidence of tying labour through land-lease contract has been insignificant.

The percentage of households who have taken institutional loans has been higher in the case of the recorded tenants although, in terms of per borrowing household availability of total credit from institutional sources, they lag behind the unrecorded tenants slightly. Quite a substantial percentage of households still depend on non-institutional sources of finance and they often obtain such loan on onerous terms. Yet, the available evidence does not provide outright support to the view that the recorded tenants have not been provided with the alternative credit support which has become essential with the non-availability of credit from the landlords. Our data clearly indicate that the credit market in our study area is clearly dominated by the non-landlord loan-givers.

6

Tenancy Contracts, Inputs Use and Productivity

Having analysed several facets of changing tenancy relations in West Bengal in the preceding chapters, we shall concentrate in this one on the issues relating to the impact of tenancy on resources use and productivity. In this context, our first main objective would be to examine whether tenancy really makes an impact on the economic performance of the households. Before we do so, we would briefly discuss some other aspects of production structure of our sample households such as asset endowment, irrigation structure and cropping pattern. We would also take note of the distribution of 'total returns' from crop production between the landlords and tenants in our study area.

Farm Asset Endowment

Some idea about the level of farm asset endowment of the sample households can be formed by analysing information gathered on the values of their owned implements and machinery and draught animals. We provide the values of implements and machinery under two heads—traditional and improved.[1] The value of implements added to the value of draught animals gives us the value of total farm assets.

Table 6.1 provides data on farm asset holdings of the unrecorded and the recorded tenants. The important points emerging from

[1] Improved implements include irrigation equipment, sprayers, threshers and so on while traditional implements include such items as ploughs, harrows, yokes and scythes, and such other implements.

Table 6.1
Farm Asset Endowment of Tenant Households (in Rupees)

Size Group (in acres)	Implements & machinery				Draught animals		Total assets	
	Traditional		Improved					
	Per farm	Per acre	Per farm	Per acre	Per farm	Per acre	Per farm	Per acre
A. UNRECORDED TENANTS								
Less than 1.00	161.45	270.78	264.45	435.76	405.53	699.87	831.43	1406.41
1.00–2.49	323.28	198.71	457.78	271.33	1276.97	776.84	2058.03	1246.88
2.50–4.99	616.03	184.24	3219.43	954.32	2496.36	746.81	6331.82	1885.37
5.00 & above	654.70	119.36	6024.00	1056.84	3700.00	662.69	10378.70	1838.89
Overall	318.01	194.41	999.34	609.25	1238.35	732.08	2555.70	1535.74
B. RECORDED TENANTS								
Less than 1.00	133.61	222.71	22.33	35.88	375.93	621.27	531.87	879.86
1.00–2.49	363.05	227.29	271.46	176.00	1264.19	799.06	1898.70	1202.35
2.50–4.99	535.45	160.18	1011.00	304.07	2081.51	618.13	3627.96	1082.38
5.00 & above	618.00	104.11	1788.00	227.20	1441.07	695.57	3847.07	1026.88
Overall	309.64	192.51	369.90	213.49	1177.19	688.89	1856.73	1094.89

the table are: first, tenant households in smaller size classes seem to have a higher per acre value of traditional implements and machinery while the per acre value of improved implements and machinery is higher in the case of households in higher farm size categories. This appears to be true for both the unrecorded and the recorded tenants. Second, there does not seem to exist any systematic relationship between per acre value of draught animals and the size of farm. Third, for all categories of tenants (unrecorded and recorded), there exists a direct relationship between farm size and per farm value of total assets. Value of total farm assets per acre, however, reveals no systematic relationship with farm size although the tenant households in higher farm size groups generally seem to have higher per acre value of total assets. Fourth, the unrecorded tenants seem to have higher per farm as well as per acre values of agricultural implements and machinery (both improved and traditional). The same is true of per farm/per acre value of draught animals. As regards per farm/per acre value of total assets too, the unrecorded tenants seem to enjoy a superiority over the recorded tenants. On the whole, our data on farm asset endowment of the households depict a superior position for the unrecorded tenants compared with their recorded counterparts.

Cropping Pattern

In this section, we examine the relationship, if any, between tenancy and cropping pattern. For this purpose, we look into how the tenant households allocate their owned, sharecropped and fixed-rented areas into various crops.[2] Our analysis is carried out separately for the two groups of tenants—unrecorded and recorded.

Table 6.2 presents data on cropping pattern for the two categories of tenants. It seems that for all types of land (owned and leased-in), Aman paddy and Boro paddy predominate in the cropping pattern. Nevertheless, owned plots of the tenant households seem to represent relatively higher percentage of area under high-value commercial crops such as jute, potatoes, sugarcane and vegetables

---

[2] In our discussion of cropping pattern, we have considered only the major crops of our study area. In that way, our discussion is not exhaustive as many other crops (mostly minor) have been left out.

Table 6.2
Cropping Pattern of Tenant Households

Type of land	Proportion of cropped area under							
	Aman Paddy	Aus Paddy	Boro Paddy	Jute	Potato	Vegetables (winter)	Sugarcane	Total
A. Unrecorded Tenants								
Owned	53.43	1.34	28.46	9.12	4.15	1.87	1.63	100.00
Leased-in								
(a) Sharecropped	44.46	0.47	44.94	6.20	2.92	0.34	0.67	100.00
(b) Fixed-rented	0.95	–	91.64	0.82	1.06	4.55	0.98	100.00
(c) Total	37.02	0.39	52.69	5.31	2.61	0.98	1.00	100.00
B. Recorded Tenants								
Owned	50.83	2.72	29.32	9.51	2.98	1.08	3.56	100.00
Leased-in								
(a) Sharecropped	58.61	1.27	31.94	3.32	0.89	0.90	3.07	100.00
(b) Fixed-rented	52.94	–	39.18	2.63	1.15	2.86	1.24	100.00
(c) Total	57.44	1.08	34.17	3.24	0.94	1.23	2.90	100.00

as compared to their leased-in plots. This implies that ownership cultivation while leading to diversification of cropping pattern also induces the households to devote larger areas under commercial crops.[3] As regards the newly emerging crop such as Boro paddy, the proportion of cropped area is, however, higher on leased-in land than on owned land. This is not surprising in so far as there has been a tendency for tenancy to assume a seasonal character in our study area whereby some households enter into the tenancy contracts exclusively for the Boro season or lease-in additional land for Boro cultivation on varying tenancy terms.

Another point to note is that the two groups of tenants do not differ systematically as regards cropping pattern on their respective owned lands. Thus, while the unrecorded tenants seem to devote a greater percentage of their owned area to specific commercial crops (such as, potatoes and other vegetables), the recorded tenants do so in respect of others (jute and sugarcane). Some difference in cropping pattern is, however, discernible in respect of their leased-in lands. It is observed from the table that while the recorded tenants have a much higher percentage of leased-in area devoted to Aman paddy, the percentage of cropped area under Boro paddy is distinctly higher on leased in plots of the unrecorded tenants. There is also some evidence, though not very strong, of the unrecorded tenants allocating higher percentage of leased in area to some commercial crops (for instance, jute and potatoes). All these facts seem to indicate that the tenanted lands of the unrecorded tenants are represented by a relatively more diversified cropping pattern while the recorded tenants are confined more to the traditional cropping systems. Such difference in cropping pattern with respect to leased-in plots of the two categories of tenants is again to be understood in terms of seasonal character of tenancy in our study area. The cropping pattern of the unrecorded tenants appears to be more diversified as they have been more successful in leasing in larger areas during the Rabi/Boro season.

Table 6.2 also provides separate information on the cropping pattern adopted by the tenant households for their sharecropped and fixed-rent portions of leased-in land. The main point to emerge

---

[3] Bharadwaj (1974: 55) also observes on the basis of Farm Management Survey data for Punjab that the proportion of cropped area under cash crops is higher on the ownership holdings as compared to tenanted holdings.

in this context is that both Aman paddy and Boro paddy predominate on the sharecropped land of all categories of tenants. On the other hand, the fixed-rent land of the unrecorded tenants is occupied largely by Boro paddy. In the case of recorded tenants, however, both Aman paddy and Boro paddy gain importance on their fixed-rent land.

Our discussion of the cropping pattern of the tenant households adopted for individual plots of land leads to the following broad conclusions: First, in as much as the tenant households report relatively more diversified cropping pattern for the owned portions of their land compared to tenanted land, ownership cultivation does provide greater incentive to adopt more rational crop combination. Second, although the unrecorded and the recorded tenants do not differ much in respect of cropping pattern adopted for their owned portions of land, there seems to exist some difference in cropping pattern with respect to their tenanted land. While the recorded tenants have remained relatively more confined to traditional cropping system, the unrecorded tenants have been more successful towards devoting higher proportion of their tenanted area to some commercial crops (including the newly emerging Boro paddy crop).

Irrigation Base

We have information on the percentage of total cropped area irrigated, as well as its source-wise distribution, for various plots of land of the tenant households. Table 6.3 presents information on the percentage of cropped area irrigated for the two categories of tenants. The main point to emerge from the table is that, in the case of the unrecorded tenants in our area, the percentage of irrigated cropped area is lower on their own land compared to that on their leased-in land (considering both the seasons together). On the other hand, in the case of the recorded tenants, the percentage of irrigated area seems to be slightly greater on their own land compared to their leased-in land. The comparison of the two groups of tenants thus shows that the tenanted land of the unrecorded tenants is relatively better irrigated than that of the recorded tenants. This is so because the former are able to draw

Table 6.3
Proportion and Source-wise Distribution of Irrigated Cropped
Area of Tenant Households

Type of land	Season	Proportion of cropped area irrigated	Proportion of irrigated area under:			
			Pumpset/ STW	DTW/ RLI	Canal	Pond/ Tank
A. UNRECORDED TENANTS						
Owned	Kharif	11.28	58.50	–	–	41.50
	Rabi/Boro	93.84	63.80	16.94	17.43	1.83
	All	42.86	63.22	15.11	15.55	6.12
Leased-in	Kharif	9.86	96.21	–	–	3.79
	Rabi/Boro	98.78	60.04	17.94	21.70	0.32
	All	60.20	62.74	16.59	20.09	0.58
B. RECORDED TENANTS						
Owned	Kharif	10.31	74.86	–	–	25.14
	Rabi/Boro	90.63	32.76	31.26	33.45	2.43
	All	42.78	37.22	28.00	29.76	5.02
Leased-in	Kharif	2.70	100.00	–	–	–
	Rabi/Boro	95.54	47.94	25.94	26.12	–
	All	40.25	49.40	25.20	25.40	–

in, as part of their seasonal arrangements, larger areas for Boro cultivation, which requires full irrigation.

Source-wise distribution of gross irrigated area for owned and leased in plots of the two categories of tenants are also given in Table 6.3. Although pumpsets and shallow tubewells (STW) are the principal sources of irrigation, a significant proportion of irrigated area is covered by pond/tank irrigation during the Kharif season. During the Boro/Rabi season, while pumpsets/STWs continue to be an important source of irrigation, a substantial part of the irrigated area is covered by improved sources, such as deep tubewells (DTW), river-lifts (RLI) and canals. It is significant that the proportion of irrigated area under these improved sources of irrigation seems to be higher for the recorded tenants (both on their own and tenanted lands) compared to the unrecorded tenants. The comparison of the two groups of tenants also shows that the unrecorded tenants have slightly higher percentage of irrigated leased-in area and a lower percentage of irrigated owned area covered under DTW/RLI and canals. This is contrary to the case with the recorded tenants.

It thus appears that not only did the unrecorded tenants report a higher proportion of leased-in area under irrigation compared with the recorded tenants, but the former also had a higher proportion of irrigated leased-in area under improved sources of irrigation (for instance, DTW/RLI and canals) during the Boro/Rabi season.

Resource-Use and Productivity

In this section, we examine the resource-use pattern and productivity level under alternative tenurial arrangements. In Chapter 1, we touched upon the debate concerning the impact of share-crop tenancy on utilization of inputs and the level of productivity/efficiency. On the theoretical plane, the traditional (Marshallian) view postulated that crop-sharing tenancy was inefficient owing to the share tenant's application of fewer variable inputs on his tenanted land resulting in lower output per unit of land. The opposite (modern or Cheungian) view is that, in a situation where the landlord can stipulate the effort to be made by the tenant on rented land, productive efficiency prevails, so that the marginal product of factors of production is equalized across lands that are owned or tenanted, whether on a crop-sharing or a fixed-rent basis. As we noted earlier, the debate is as yet inconclusive. Even the empirical studies conducted to test the resource allocation pattern and productivity level under crop-sharing tenancy do not greatly help us to arrive at a general conclusion on the subject. As a matter of fact, most of the empirical studies suffer from inadequate data base and/or adopt improper methodology and hence cannot be relied upon. Before we present our own observations on resource use pattern and productivity level under tenant cultivation, it would be befitting to have a brief look at some major problems which have plagued previous studies on the subject.

A close look into the arguments of Marshall and Cheung concerning resource-use efficiency under crop-sharing tenancy reflects that one of the fundamental ways in which Cheung differs from the Marshallians is that he clearly recognises the role of landlords' monitoring/supervision as a corrective towards tenancy inefficiency (Cheung, 1969: Ch. II). The main spirit of Cheung's argument has been that, with the landlord showing active interest by stipulating and enforcing the required level of effort but also actively participating in decision-making and cost-sharing, agricultural operations become a joint venture between him and the tenant. It is this kind of arrangement which might lead to removal of inefficiency under tenant cultivation, if any. Unfortunately, most of the empirical studies supporting Cheung's equal-efficiency argument are preoccupied with the comparison of per acre inputs use and productivity level under alternative cultivation forms and do not spell out clearly the mechanism which makes the establishment of equal-efficiency in actual situations—whether it is because of contract enforcement by the landlord or the landlord's committed supervision or cost-sharing. One way of ascertaining the contributory roles, if any, of these factors in removing the inefficiency of tenant cultivation is to compare the cases where the landlord monitors the process of cultivation (through input stipulation, supervision, cost-sharing and such like instruments) with cases where the landlord does not. To the extent that most of the researchers do not distinguish between these varying cases, their studies do not strictly provide an appropriate framework for testing of Cheung's hypothesis.[4]

Further, one encounters some ambiguity in the definition of categories such as 'owners' and 'tenants'. While some scholars include in the category of tenants all those who lease in land irrespective of whether they also possess some land of their own (see Rao, 1971: 588), others construct an index representing the proportion of leased-in area to total cultivated area so as to determine the status of the households in the rural economy (see Chakravarty and Rudra, 1973). The latter procedure actually ends with groupings of the class of mixed tenants (i.e. owner-cum-tenants) into 'owners' and 'sharecroppers'. Consequently, the studies based on such a procedure cannot be relied upon as true testing of the efficiency of tenant cultivation.[5]

Another important drawback with many empirical studies is that

[4] One recent exception in this context is the study conducted by Nabi (1986: 429–42) in ten villages in Khanewal sub-division of Pakistan's Punjab. He shows how cost-sharing and direct supervision of landlords ensure efficiency in resource allocation under sharecropping. However, to put the record straight, even his study does not satisfactorily provide for direct comparison between cost-sharing and non-cost-sharing or landlord supervision and non-supervision cases so as to bring out the impact of these factors on resource-use efficiency of the tenants.

[5] Commenting upon such a procedure of classification of the households, Shaban writes: '(*with this procedure*) it is not difficult to generate data that are consistent with the Marshallian specification of labour allocation and at the same time would justify the conclusions of these studies that "owners" and "sharecroppers" have similar inputs and outputs per unit area.' See Shaban (1987: 914), italics added.

they are content to compare the resource use of the pure owners and the tenants.[6] The fact remains that the category of tenants does not constitute a homogeneous class and there could be differences even among themselves depending upon the form of tenancy (such as sharecropping tenancy and fixed-rent tenancy). Although some of these studies relate to the regions dominated by crop-sharing tenancy, their analyses are nonetheless inadequate if one is interested in looking into the comparative behaviour of alternative tenancy arrangements (Shaban, 1987: 913).

There is also the problem associated with the aggregation of various crops cultivated on a given plot of land. While examining differences in input use and productivity level between owner-operated and tenant-operated farms, most of the studies remain confined to comparisons, of their performance in crop production (that is, considering all crops cultivated on a given plot together). This is inappropriate in so far as it fails to explain whether observed differences in resource use and productivity between owned and tenanted lands are because of differences in cropping patterns or due to the disincentive effect of tenant cultivation. In the general case, owned land being available for cultivation round the year might induce the cultivation of high value commercial crops (which also require higher doses of labour and non-labour inputs) on a greater scale compared to tenanted lands cultivated on seasonal basis or confined to a traditional cropping system. Under these circumstances, a comparison of performances of owners and tenants in crop production would almost invariably depict the former as more efficient.

The other problem relates to the selection of an appropriate statistical procedure for testing the significance of differences in performance under alternative forms of cultivation. A large number of studies employed Fisher's t-test to examine the significance of difference in input utilization and productivity level between the owners and the tenants. As is well-known, this is a fairly rigorous test for comparison of mean values for two samples if the underlying distribution in two samples is normal and there is common within-sample variance. Even with population distributions not being too close to normal, the test could still work satisfactorily,

<hr />

[6] Some of the studies to suffer from this limitation are Chakravarty and Rudra (1973); Dwivedi and Rudra (1973) and Chattopadhyay (1979).

provided the sample sizes are large (about twenty or more) (Manly; 1986: 27). The problem of unequal within-sample variance is also not too serious provided the ratio of true variances is within the limits 0.4 and 2.5 (*ibid.*).[7] However, the greatest problem with most of the empirical studies using this test procedure is that they suffer from inadequate sample size.[8]

There have also been some attempts to test the differences in performance of the same household on his owned and tenanted portions of land (see Bell, 1977; Nabi, 1986). Testing the performance of the same individual across his owned and tenanted plots provides powerful testing of tenancy inefficiency, if any. However, even the studies relying on this procedure very often suffer from data limitations.[9]

Having noted the main problems associated with past studies on the issue of efficiency of the households under alternative tenurial arrangements, we can now set out our own framework for testing the same in our study area. We have noted in Chapter 5 that the incidence of cost-sharing has not been very high among the landlords for all categories of tenants and all decisions concerning production are taken by the tenants themselves. Further, there is no evidence of landlords making stipulations of inputs for the rented lands. In other words, the situation resembles one of ineffective monitoring. In this situation, any evidence of inefficiency of tenant cultivation could be related to 'pure disincentive effect' on the tenant households emanating from their lack of ownership rights.

In order to avoid confusion arising out of definition of tenants and to provide vigour to the test of efficiency under tenant cultivation, we have directly compared the performance of the same set of households in their owned and their tenanted land. This is facilitated by the fact that our sample actually constituted a fairly broad mixture of owner-cum-tenants (the incidence of pure tenants has been very low). Thanks again to fairly wide number of situations

---

[7] In order to tackle the problem of unequal within-sample variances, Dwivedi and Rudra (1973: 1293) make some adjustment to computed t-values by using a test procedure due to Cochran.

[8] The studies to suffer from severe inadequacy of sample size are Chakravarty and Rudra (1973); Dwivedi and Rudra (1973) and Nabi (1986).

[9] The studies using this procedure but suffering from inadequate sample size are Dwivedi and Rudra (1973) and Nabi (1986).

available in our sample data, we also make a distinction between crop-sharing and fixed-rent contracts in order to bring into focus households' performances under alternative tenancy arrangements. The analysis is carried out at the disaggregated level for individual crops as well as for all crops taken together.

Since our data set allows us to test the differences in resource allocation and productivity level by the same households among their various plots of land (owned, sharecropped and so on), we can do the same by using the Paired-t test. To the extent that the performance of an owner-cum-tenant on his sharecropped/fixed rent plot is not independent of that on his owned plot (stated in other language, two samples representing performances on owned plots and sharecropped/fixed rent plots are not completely independent), the Paired-t offers a suitable procedure for testing if the households actually discriminate between various plots under their cultivation.[10] This test has an added advantage that with number of observations between two samples being equal, it becomes more vigorous as a procedure for testing the differences in means between two samples.

The differences in the performances of the households across various plots of land are examined by considering data on four important variables: (*a*) material inputs per acre (Rs.); (*b*) bullock labour per acre (pair-days); (*c*) human labour per acre (man-days); and (*d*) output per acre (Rs.). The main objective is to see whether the performance of the households (as represented by these four variables) differs between their owned and sharecropped/fixed rented plots.[11]

[10] The formula for the Paired-t-test is:

$$t = \frac{(\bar{x}_i - \bar{x}_j) / n}{\text{S.D. of } (x_i - x_j)}$$

with n–1 degree of freedom where $\bar{x}_j$ and $\bar{x}_i$ are mean values for two samples x_i and x_j (i, j = 1, 2, . . . , n).

[11] It may be noted that some scholars have also attempted to judge the allocative efficiency of the alternative tenancy arrangements by applying the neoclassical production function technique (see, for example, Bagi; 1981). The difficulties of such a procedure are, however, very well documented (see, in this context, Bharadwaj, 1980; Junankar, 1989). We have confined ourselves to the examination of the differences in economic performance (as revealed by some important performance variables) between owned and leased-in plots of land of the class of owner-cum-tenants. This provides some idea about the impact that tenancy makes on allocation/utilization of resources and productivity level in the study region.

Owned Plots versus Sharecropped Plots

We first examine the differences in economic performances of the class of owner-cum-share tenants in our study area. To be precise, we compare the performance between their owned and share-cropped plots. This would enable us to form an idea about the difference that crop-sharing tenancy makes on resource-use and productivity levels. The analysis is carried out chronologically for the traditional crop Aman paddy, newly emerging crop Boro (summer) paddy, cash crops (comprising jute, potato and sugar-cane) and, finally, for all crops taken together.

It is observed from Table 6.4 that in respect of the traditional crop, Aman paddy, the unrecorded tenants use more material inputs and human labour on their owned plots rather than their sharecropped plots. They also have a higher per acre output on the former plots of land. All these differences are found to be statistically significant. The situation for the recorded tenants is somewhat similar to that observed for the unrecorded tenants. It clearly emerges that the recorded tenants use a greater amount of all inputs and obtain a higher productivity level for Aman paddy on their owned plots rather than their sharecropped plots. The differ-ences in resources use and productivity level are all statistically significant.

We may observe that all categories of tenants tend to use higher doses of inputs and have the benefit of higher productivity levels from their owned plots compared to their sharecropped plots in the case of traditional crop Aman paddy. To the extent that the differences in. input utilization and productivity levels between these plots of land turn out to be significant in most of the cases, the system of ownership cultivation may be viewed as more efficient in terms of resource allocation vis-à-vis the system of crop-sharing for the traditional crop, Aman paddy.

Let us turn to the newly emerging crop Boro paddy. It is observed that the unrecorded tenants maintain a superior per-formance on their owned plots for this newly emerging crop as well. As is clear in Table 6.4, the utilization of all inputs and the productivity level are both significantly higher on the owned plots of the unrecorded tenants compared to their sharecropped plots. The situation is, however, slightly different for the recorded tenants. Table 6.4 shows that there exists no significant difference

Table 6.4
Comparison of Economic Performance on Owned Plots (x_1) versus Sharecropped Plots (x_2)

Crop	Performance criterion	Unrecorded tenants			Recorded tenants		
		$\bar{x}_1$	$\bar{x}_2$	t-value	$\bar{x}_1$	$\bar{x}_2$	t-value
Aman Paddy	M	449.18	240.62	2.23**	337.19	267.00	4.05*
($n_1 = 60$	B	12.20	12.30	−0.14	14.35	13.53	1.68**
$n_2 = 65$)	H	83.49	62.14	2.42*	71.85	66.90	1.56***
	O	2449.10	1864.27	1.89**	2074.54	1934.98	1.30***
Boro Paddy	M	764.93	742.84	1.58****	729.87	699.79	1.04
($n_1 = 58$	B	10.90	10.00	1.75***	13.57	14.43	−0.83
$n_2 = 27$)	H	119.76	114.57	1.96***	109.04	111.82	−0.88
	O	3407.87	3092.64	3.65*	3365.94	3324.83	0.24
Jute	M	176.88	158.48	0.72	203.28	270.28	−1.41***
($n_1 = 16$	B	10.81	10.58	0.54	14.17	13.63	0.40
$n_2 = 10$)	H	105.86	105.91	−0.01	110.12	100.76	1.25
	O	1944.78	2002.81	−0.37	1369.68	1449.00	−0.47
Potato	M	3505.46	3514.40	−0.27	2958.75	2910.00	1.35
($n_1 = 9$	B	16.23	18.36	−1.49***	15.00	12.92	1.41
$n_2 = 2$)	H	84.77	80.46	1.85***	83.75	80.42	5.66***
	O	8148.15	7535.56	1.08	7600.00	8012.50	−1.41
Sugarcane	M	961.13	922.33	0.53	438.16	350.74	−1.17
($n_1 = 7$	B	13.95	12.81	0.51	7.19	10.53	−2.05***
$n_2 = 4$)	H	238.29	252.20	−0.38	244.36	239.56	0.09
	O	5255.62	6952.26	−1.41	4020.15	4072.19	−0.11

All Crops (n₁ = 112, n₂ = 83)						
M	688.02	579.68	1.99**	566.63	453.56	3.85*
B	11.83	11.29	1.33***	13.74	13.31	1.04
H	109.16	100.44	2.06**	101.12	85.80	1.80**
O	3209.87	2853.97	1.79**	2657.23	2438.74	2.16**

Notes: 1. M = material inputs per acre (Rs.); B = bullock labour per acre (in pair-days); H = human labour per acre (in mandays); O = Output per acre (Rs.).

2. n_1 and n_2 denote the number of pairs for unrecorded and recorded tenants respectively.

3. *, ** and *** imply significance at 1, 5 and 10 per cent level respectively.

in respect of utilization of inputs and productivity level between their owned and sharecropped plots for Boro paddy.

A comparison of the two groups of tenants reveals that, for the newly emerging crop Boro paddy also, the unrecorded tenants continue to show a superior performance (measured through the resource-use pattern and productivity level) on their owned plots vis-à-vis their sharecropped plots, while the recorded tenants do not discriminate much between these alternative plots under cultivation.

The pattern of resource allocation and productivity level under these alternative plots of land for some cash crops of our study area are also shown in Table 6.4. Here, we consider three major commercial crops, viz., jute, potatoes and sugarcane. The main point to emerge from the table is that there is no systematic and significant difference as regards the utilization of inputs and productivity level between the owned and sharecropped plots of the tenant households (both unrecorded and recorded) for such crops. It is, however, to be admitted that the testing of difference in performance between these alternative plots of land is carried out with fewer observations and need not be considered as definitive as in the case of Aman and Boro paddy.[12]

We are now ready to look into the economic performance of the two groups of tenants on their owned and sharecropped lands considering all crops together. Table 6.4 shows that the unrecorded tenants report a significantly higher utilization of all inputs as well as productivity level on their owned plots compared with the sharecropped plots. The situation is somewhat similar with the recorded tenants so that the per acre utilization of all inputs (except bullock labour) as well as the productivity level turn out to be significantly higher on their owned plots in respect of the total for all crops.

Owned versus Fixed-rent Plots

We now compare the performances of our tenant households over their owned and fixed-rent plots. We adopt a similar procedure

[12] This is mainly because crop-sharing tenancy has been largely confined to the cultivation of Aman paddy and Boro paddy in our study area. Moreover, we have considered only those cases where we could form pairs of observations between owned and sharecropped plots.

Table 6.5
Comparison of Economic Performance on Owned Plots (x_1) versus Fixed-rented Plots (x_2)

Crop	Performance criterion	Unrecorded tenants			Recorded tenants		
		$\bar{x}_1$	$\bar{x}_2$	t-value	$\bar{x}_1$	$\bar{x}_2$	t-value
Boro Paddy ($n_1 = 22$, $n_2 = 5$)	M	825.72	804.56	1.25	674.10	630.93	0.58
	B	8.92	9.48	-0.67	11.86	10.85	1.83***
	H	98.43	96.13	0.94	96.93	102.01	-2.34**
	O	3816.77	3619.07	1.25	3110.18	3119.94	-0.18
All Crops ($n_1 = 34$, $n_2 = 11$)	M	1155.78	1090.15	0.41	513.62	683.62	-0.83
	B	11.15	9.30	1.19	12.96	11.80	0.80
	H	125.08	141.52	-0.80	99.57	103.49	-0.21
	O	5155.31	4970.50	0.31	2944.05	3123.71	-0.29

Notes: As in Table 6.4.

and consider the same set of performance variables as before. Since fixed-rent tenancy is confined largely to the cultivation of Boro paddy, for crop-level analysis, we concentrate our attention on this crop only. Of course, the comparison is extended at the level of total crop output also.

Table 6.5 presents test results concerning the differences in the performance on owned plots and fixed-rent plots for the two categories of tenants. It clearly emerges from the table that, contrary to the case with crop-sharing contracts, the performance of the households under fixed-rent plots does not differ significantly from that on their owned plots. This is true of both categories of tenants (unrecorded and recorded) cultivating Boro paddy under fixed-rent contracts. Even for all crops (under fixed-rent tenancy) taken together there is no clear evidence of households discriminating between their owned and fixed-rented lands. The intensity of resource use as well as productivity level appear to be invariant between owned and fixed-rent plots.

Operation Barga: Production Gain or Loss?

The preceding discussion provided some evidence of tenants—both unrecorded and recorded—using smaller quantities of inputs and obtaining lower levels of output per acre under crop-sharing contracts compared to the outputs under ownership cultivation. This being so, one may naturally ask: to what extent has the programme of Operation Barga (O.B.) contributed in terms of actual gain in production? In as much as O.B. provides legal protection to the recorded tenants against eviction and rent-enhancement by their landlords, along with the provision of credit support from institutional agencies, one may expect *a priori* that the recorded tenants come up with better economic performance even on their share-cropped lands. If, however, the recorded tenants are observed to practise a differential pattern of resource allocation between their owned and sharecropped plots even after recording, it might lead one to believe that the O.B. programme has not had any impact in terms of gain in production. To put it more forcefully, it might even be construed to mean that the O.B. programme has actually led to production loss in West Bengal. In our opinion, however, such reasoning appears over-simplistic and cannot be sustained on the following grounds.

First, if the tenants apply more inputs and obtain a higher productivity level on their owned lands compared to those for sharecropped lands even after recording, one need not cast doubt on the merit of the O.B programme. After all, giving some legal protection to the share tenant on his leased-in land is not the same as offering him the ownership right on the same land. Naturally, there could still be disincentives associated with the former so that the tenants might place their owned plots higher in their order of preference than their sharecropped plots for the allocation of resources even after recording. In other words, recording the names of bargadars may not necessarily remove the inefficiency of resource allocation which flows from the very nature of the crop-sharing arrangement (that is, where every gain in production owing to additional effort by the tenant would automatically get shared with the landlord in proportior agreed upon).

Second, the very argument that barga recording results in actual loss of production in West Bengal cannot be accepted, at least until one proves that the performance of the recorded tenants on their sharecropped land is worse than the performance of the unrecorded tenants on the same set of plots.

The data available with us enable the comparison of the performance of the two groups of tenants on their respective sharecropped lands. Before we compare them, we should ascertain if there exists any difference in their performance on owned plots. Unlike in our previous exercise, we consider all owned plots and sharecropped plots. Thus, a nousehold having some owned area cultivated under the chosen crop would be included in the sample for owned plots irrespective of whether the same crop is cultivated on his sharecropped land and vice versa.[13] The significance of difference in performance between owned/sharecropped plots of the two groups of tenants (that is, recorded against unrecorded) is

---

[13] We could also use the same data set used above for conducting Paired-t test. However, the present one comprises bigger samples since it includes all owned plots/sharecropped plots of the households. Further, on examination it is found that there is not much difference in test results whichever data set we make use of for examining the performances of the two groups of households between their owned/sharecropped plots.

tested by using Fisher's t-test.[14] The analysis is carried out for two most important crops involving crop-sharing arrangements in our study area—Aman paddy and Boro paddy.

Table 6.6 shows test results. It may be observed that, as regards Aman paddy, there is not much evidence of systematic difference in the utilization of inputs as well as productivity level between the owned plots of the two groups of tenants. Even for Boro paddy, there is no systematic pattern, although the unrecorded tenants put significantly higher doses of at least two important inputs (material inputs and human labour) per acre on their owned plots compared with the recorded tenants. It, therefore, appears that, in general, there is no very significant difference in the performance of the two categories of tenants on their respective owned plots for the traditional crop, Aman paddy, as well as for the newly emerging crop, Boro paddy.

As regards the performance of the two groups of tenants on their sharecropped plots, Table 6.6 shows that the recorded tenants report a higher utilization of all inputs and gain a higher productivity level on their sharecropped lands compared with the unrecorded tenants in the case of Aman paddy. The differences are also statistically significant in most of the cases (except output per acre). For Boro paddy, however, no systematic pattern emerges. While the unrecorded tenants use significantly higher doses of material inputs on their sharecropped land, the recorded tenants do so in respect of bullock labour. As regards the utilization of human labour and the productivity level, no significant difference is discernible between the sharecropped plots of the two categories of tenants.

Our discussion shows that for the traditional crop, Aman paddy, the two categories of tenants do not differ greatly in terms of utilization of inputs and productivity levels on their respective

---

[14] The formula for Fisher's t is:

$$ t = \frac{\bar{x}_1 - \bar{x}_2}{S \sqrt{\dfrac{1}{n_1} + \dfrac{1}{n_2}}} $$

with $n_1 + n_2 - 2$ degree of freedom where
$$ S^2 = [(n_1 - 1) s^2_1 + (n_2 - 1) s^2_2] / (n_1 + n_2 - 2) $$

Table 6.6
Test for Differences in Economic Performance on Owned/Sharecropped
Plots of Unrecorded (x_1) and Recorded (x_2) Tenants

Performance criterion	Tenant type	Owned plots		Sharecropped plots	
		Aman paddy	Boro paddy	Aman paddy	Boro paddy
M	x_1	344.14	789.88	235.97	735.74
	x_2	320.25	724.81	266.27	694.73
	t	0.82	2.20**	-1.51***	1.32***
B	x_1	12.52	10.74	12.19	10.16
	x_2	14.25	13.85	13.62	13.95
	t	-3.26*	-4.19*	-2.27**	-5.09*
H	x_1	68.35	115.57	60.47	113.79
	x_2	70.02	108.31	69.33	112.24
	t	-0.41	1.38***	-1.69**	0.35
O	x_1	2118.35	3489.39	1760.57	3191.23
	x_2	2008.57	3397.18	1907.01	3216.23
	t	0.98	0.86	-1.25	-0.18
Number of x_1		97	83	97	96
Number of x_2		83	53	83	56
Degree of freedom		178	134	178	150

Notes: As in Table 6.4.

owned plots, there is indeed some difference in their performance in respect of the sharecropped plots. Actually, for Aman paddy, the performance of the recorded tenants is found to be better on their sharecropped plots compared with the performance on the sharecropped plots by the unrecorded tenants. On the other hand, for Boro paddy, there does not seem to exist any systematic difference in performance either between owned plots or share-cropped plots of the two categories of tenants. To the extent that the recorded tenants seem to perform better on their sharecropped plots, compared with performance of the unrecorded tenants on similar plots for the most important crop of our study area (Aman paddy), and also that their performance has not been too different with respect to the other crop (Boro paddy), our data do not lend any support to the view that the launching of O.B. has resulted in the loss of production in West Bengal.

Distribution of Total Returns

It is also necessary to examine the pattern of distribution of total returns from rented lands between the tenants and landowners. What is important to both the parties is how the ultimate gains/losses from cultivation get distributed between them. Keeping this in mind, we examine the pattern of distribution of total returns from the sharecropped plots between the two groups of tenants and their landowners. This would also facilitate examining the proposition put forward by some scholars that the bargadars (sharecroppers) have suffered loss of income following the recording of their names under O.B.[15]

'Total returns' from production of a given crop (under crop-sharing) is obtained by deducting all paid-out costs as well as imputed values of all inputs contributed by the tenant's family (except human labour) from the total value of gross output. The tenant's share in 'total returns' is the difference between 'total returns' and net rent paid (that is, total rent received by the landlord minus his share in the cost of production). In fact, the tenant's share in 'total returns' resembles a return to his family labour spent on crop production, maintenance of his own bullocks as well as his own capital.

The pattern of distribution of 'total returns' from Aman paddy and Boro paddy between the two categories of tenants and their landlords is shown in Table 6.7. It appears that the share of rent in 'total returns' is much higher in the case of the landlords of the unrecorded tenants in our study area for the traditional Aman paddy crop. The unrecorded tenants could actually retain, as their share, merely 32 per cent of the 'total returns' from Aman paddy, while the corresponding figure for the recorded tenants turns out to be as high as 59 per cent. The same pattern continues as regards distribution of 'total returns' from the sharecropped lands under Boro paddy. As shown in Table 6.7, the unrecorded tenants receive a strikingly lower proportion of 'total returns' from their share-cropped lands (nearly 35 per cent), compared to that received by the recorded tenants (62 per cent).

---

[15] This is the view put forward most vociferously by Rudra (1981: A65) but without any empirical evidence.

Table 6.7
Distribution of Total Returns from Sharecropped Plots

Item	Aman paddy		Boro paddy	
	UR	R	UR	R
Gross output per acre (Rs.)	1760.57	1907.01	3191.23	3216.24
Total returns per acre (Rs.)	1254.27	1099.94	1390.00	1425.73
Tenant's share in total returns:				
(a) per acre (Rs.)	403.21	651.99	483.18	879.28
(b) per cent to total	32.15	59.28	34.76	61.68
(c) per family manday				
employed (Rs.)	9.27	13.41	5.76	11.99
(d) returns after deducting				
imputed wages for family				
labour (Rs.)	−73.69	98.80	−454.26	−25.07
Rent per acre (Rs.)	851.06	447.95	906.82	546.45
Rent as per cent of total				
returns (Rs.)	67.85	40.72	65.24	38.32

Note: UR = Unrecorded; R = Recorded.

It appears, therefore, that the recorded tenants are able to extract a much larger share of 'total returns' which surely contributes to an augmentation of their incomes. Actually, the higher share of total returns accrues to them through a better exercise of their crop-sharing rights, as a consequence of O.B. On this count, one may effectively challenge the viewpoint that barga recording has led to a loss of income of the bargadars.

The examination on the asset endowments of the unrecorded and the recorded tenants revealed a superior position for the former in our study area. The unrecorded tenants seem to have higher per acre values of draught animals as well as total assets. The tenanted lands of the unrecorded tenants also appear to be better irrigated. This is because the unrecorded tenants are able to attract, as part of their seasonal arrangements, larger areas for Boro cultivation, which is fully irrigated. As regards cropping patterns, all categories of tenants are found to devote a relatively higher percentage of owned area to high-value commercial crops compared with their leased-in lands. Between the two groups of tenants, the unrecorded tenants appear to have a slightly higher percentage of leased-in area under commercial crops (including Boro paddy), while the recorded tenants being relatively more confined to the traditional cropping system on their leased-in plots.

Analysing the patterns of input utilization and productivity level under alternative plots of lands, we observe a tendency on the part of all categories of tenants (unrecorded and recorded) to apply higher doses of inputs and obtain better productivity levels on their owned plots compared to their sharecropped plots. This signifies the misallocative behaviour of crop-sharing tenancy vis-à-vis the system of ownership cultivation in our study area. We, however, encountered no significant difference in the performance of the households (both unrecorded and recorded) between their owned and fixed-rent plots.

There is no significant difference between the performances (as revealed by per acre utilization of inputs and productivity level) of the unrecorded and the recorded tenants on their owned plots. However, as regards the performance on sharecropped plots, the recorded tenants seem to display a better position. With the recorded tenants performing better or at least at levels competitive to those of the unrecorded tenants on their sharecropped plots, our data do not lend support to the view that Operation Barga has led to loss of production in West Bengal.

Finally, the pattern of distribution of 'total returns' between the tenants and the landlords clearly reveals that the recorded tenants are able to extract a larger share of 'total returns' compared to the unrecorded tenants. This they do through better exercise of their crop-sharing rights, following the recording of names. To that extent, barga recording seems to have led to the augmentation of income of the recorded tenants.

7

Summary and Conclusions

Under the land policy adopted by the colonial rulers in Bengal, the peasants lost their customary rights over land and the erstwhile collectors of revenue, the zamindars, became the proprietors. The zamindars, instead of providing leadership towards improvements in agriculture, ruthlessly embarked extensive rent exploitation of the poor peasantry and subinfeudation grew. The misery of the peasants of Bengal accentuated with the emergence of another category of exploiters, locally called jotedars, who too took up the subletting of land and extracted heavy rents from the tenantry. As a matter of fact, much of the spread of sharecropping in colonial Bengal is related to the spread of the jotedari system. Of course, the growth of sharecropping in Bengal was due to several other factors: for instance, the increasing pressure of population on land with the destruction of indigenous manufacturing, the process of depeasantization caused by famines or the debt-burden, the creation of urban job opportunities for a section of the landowners, upper class/caste inhibitions and taboos against physical participation in agriculture, the depression of the 1930s, and the passing of tenancy laws giving occupancy status to tenants who paid fixed rents but denying the same to sharecroppers. For the landowners, share-cropping was also a preferred option because, contrary to the case of self-cultivation with hired labour, it required very little time for supervision. Moreover, the rent obtainable under crop-sharing arrangements was much higher than in fixed-rent tenancy.

The terms and conditions of sharecropping contracts during the colonial period varied, depending upon the agreement reached between the landowners and the share tenants (the arrangements being highly personalized in nature). The share of output going to the tenants generally varied between a third and a half, while input costs were mostly borne by the share tenants. The sharecropping arrangement very often led to a dependency (patron-client) relationship, with the tenant depending on the landowner for credit and supplying, *inter alia*, 'begar' (unpaid labour services) to the landowner's family. In essence, it was a blatantly unequal exchange between the two parties—the weaker party (the share tenant) being exploited by the stronger (the landowner). The exploitation was magnified when land-lease, labour and credit contracts were interlinked. The point of special importance is the almost complete reluctance of the colonial rulers to protect the interest of this weaker section—the share tenants. Although some tenancy Acts were passed during the colonial period, these were directed primarily towards safeguarding the interests of the occupancy tenants. By and large, the class of share tenants received no protection against the exploitation of the landowners, nor was any effort made to provide them occupancy status. The extremely vulnerable position of the share tenants was thus the agrarian reality that Bengal inherited from the colonial regime.

Immediately after Independence, several tenancy reform Acts were initiated. The Acts passed up to about the early seventies were purported to delineate by law the share of the crop to be retained by the tenant as well as to make tenant eviction difficult except under exceptional circumstances. The story of tenancy reform in independent Bengal till this period, however, is that of the passing of various Acts, but of no serious attempt being made to put them into effective operation at the grass-roots level. The outcome was not only the denial of the crop-sharing rights of the sharecroppers, but of many who received notional protection under the law, being evicted and/or relegated to the status of agricultural labourers. For all those years, there was hesitation at the political level about giving the sharecroppers adequate protection against the threat of eviction and rent-exploitation by the landowners.

The situation took a turn for the better with the Left Front's coming into power in 1977. The Left Front Government gave serious attention to the problem of safeguarding the interests of the weaker sections in the countryside. The cause of the sharecroppers was taken up in right earnest. There was not much legislative work left to be done; the government had only to plug the loopholes in the existing legislation and implement it in earnest. Tenancy reforms under Left Front rule actually take the shape of an organized struggle of the share tenants. The most important element in Left Front Government's package of reforms has been the launching of an organized campaign to record the names of the sharecroppers (Operation Barga) so as to give them legal protection against rent-enhancement and eviction by landowners. The benefits of institutional finance were also made available. The ultimate objective of the whole struggle was clearly to free the sharecroppers from the exploitation of landowners and money-lenders through collective effort.

The Structure and Functioning of the Tenancy System

We have analysed the National Sample Survey (N.S.S.) data so as to obtain a macro-level understanding of the changes in the structure of tenancy in West Bengal since Independence. Our main findings are the following:

1. There has been a gradual decline in the extent of tenancy cultivation in West Bengal. As per the latest available N.S.S. estimates, about 13 per cent of operated area in the state was under tenant cultivation in 1982, which is much lower than its counterpart (about 25.0 per cent) in 1953–54. The decline in tenancy cultivated area has been particularly drastic in the years since 1971–72. The reasons for such a decline might be due to the rigorous application of tenancy legislation and recent progress in agricultural technology, which have rendered self-cultivation safe and remunerative. In spite of the fact that both these factors tend to put a downward pressure on the extent of tenancy, such a low reporting of tenancy might also be due to a growing tendency towards concealment in recent years. Even if we accept, with due scepticism, the extent of tenant cultivation reported in the official documents, it would perhaps be valid to conjecture that the area under tenancy in West Bengal has reached a low-level equilibrium, from which it is unlikely to decline in the near future. With a large majority of the tenants having been mobilized to record their names (which makes tenant eviction difficult, except under extra-ordinary circumstances) and a substantial proportion of land still held by high landowning/non-cultivating categories, tenancy in the state should remain, at least for quite some time, at the extent at which it stands now.

2. Another important aspect of the changing tenancy structure in West Bengal relates to the growing preponderance of lower (mostly marginal and small) landowning/operating categories, both as lessors and lessees. This has important implications for formulating future policies for conferring ownership rights on the actual tillers of the soil. In particular, it would be interesting to see whether the Left parties in power would like to designate this bulk of low-landowning lessors as 'landlords' or 'jotedars' and give a call for their extinction at a time when all political parties are competing with one another to woo majority support purely on electoral considerations at the grass-roots level.

3. The land-lease market in West Bengal is now dominated by mixed holdings (that is, owner-cum-tenants) rather than by entirely leased-in holdings (pure tenants). This renders most of the recently developed neoclassical models on tenancy inapplicable, owing to their traditional notion that the class of tenants necessarily comprise the landless.

4. Although sharecropping continues as the predominant form of tenancy in West Bengal, there has been a tendency in recent years towards its decline, with the growing importance of fixed-rent tenancy. This possibly happens with the progress of agricultural technology (which is likely to discourage the tenant to share the benefits with the landowner through crop-sharing arrangements) as also with the growing tendency towards seasonalization of tenancy contracts (since a seasonal tenancy arrangement makes evasion of tenancy laws by the landowner easier and both the tenant and landowner show a preference for fixed-rent contracts with such arrangements). In that sense, our study foresees fixed-rent tenancy gaining more prominence in the years to come.

We have also carried out detailed field inquiries in a sample district, Midnapore, so as to obtain a better understanding of the structure and functioning of the tenancy system. The analysis of field data also brings out the impact of organization and mobilization of the tenants in recent years (as through Operation Barga) on tenurial relations in the state. In this context, we have emphasized the comparison between the unrecorded tenants (that is, the group which typically portrays the traditional tenancy arrangement) and the recorded tenants (the participants in Operation Barga). This puts to empirical scrutiny our hypothesis that the recorded tenants have started enjoying collective and organized strength and that the old tenancy relations characterized by exploitation of the tenants have started breaking up. Several interesting findings emanate from this part of our study of which a few important ones are highlighted below:

Socio-economic status of tenants: Consistent with the overall pattern for the state as a whole, our survey data depict the existence of very few pure tenants and the land-lease market is very much dominated by the category of owner-cum-tenants. Among the tenants there is a clear preponderance of marginal (less than 2.50 acres) and small (2.50–4.99 acres) owners. The two categories of tenants (unrecorded and recorded) do not differ much in terms of their economic status (as revealed by their landholding position). However, they are different in respect of social status. We observe that in comparison to the unrecorded tenants, the recorded tenants have a higher percentage of lower castes/tribals, as well as of illiterates. The recorded tenants also belong more to the traditional sharecropper-cum-agricultural labour families, in contrast to the unrecorded tenants, who are relatively new entrants in the land-lease market. In sum, our study portrays a weaker social, if not economic, status for the recorded tenants.

Socio-economic background of lessors: On the question of socio-economic status of the lessees vis-à-vis the lessors, the present study generally shows a superior position for the latter. This becomes clear from the fact that the lessors have a much higher percentage of upper-caste households and also that a substantial proportion of them belong to relatively higher land-owning categories.

Who leases from whom? Our enquiry into the distribution of lease units by lessee-lessor groups provides answers to an important question, namely, who leases from whom in the market for land-lease. This also throws up many interesting facts concerning the functioning of land-lease market:
   1. There is a tendency for smaller unrecorded lessees to lease in more from smaller lessors while the bigger lessees are preferred by the bigger lessors. The situation is somewhat different in the case of the recorded lessees, with their lessors being drawn more from relatively higher ownership categories.

2. Although both categories of lessees reported a substantial proportion of their lessors being engaged in non-agricultural activities, a strict comparison between the two groups of lessees brings out that a relatively lower proportion of the lessors of the unrecorded lessees are involved in non-agricultural activities (that is, a higher proportion is engaged in self-cultivation). The lessors having non-agricultural activities as their principal occupation prefer leasing out to unrecorded lessees of higher size-groups, while those belonging to the cultivating community look for unrecorded lessees with a small land area. In the case of recorded lessees, a greater proportion of their lessors seems to be engaged in non-agricultural activities. All these seem to suggest that primarily non-agricultural families having an additional interest in land suffered more through 'barga' recording in the areas investigated.

3. In the land-lease market, there seems to exist no tie-up between the lessee to a specific lessor. In fact, a lessee is free to enter into lease arrangements with as many lessors as he can. It is an important finding in that it signals the breaking of traditional dependence-dominance relationship between the lessee and his lessor. Between the two groups of lessees, however, the unrecorded ones are more successful in attracting a greater number of lessors presumably because of their greater 'trustworthiness'.

Motivation for leasing in: The greater availability of farm family labour in relation to owned land motivates a large section of poor (nearly landless) tenants to enter into tenancy contracts. Constrained by a limited land base of their own and uncertain labour markets, these households find no other option but to enter into tenancy arrangements if only to ensure more effective utilization of their surplus labour. This brings us to the conclusion that in a land-scarce but labour-abundant economy, tenancy serves to equalize the land-labour ratio across rural households and for that matter, tenancy would persist as long as the land-labour ratio varies among them (unless there is legal intervention to ban tenancy).

Changing technological situation and tenancy: The most important effect of the new production technology comes through changes in the form of tenancy. Thus, while sharecropping predominates during the Kharif season in our study regions, a tendency is clearly discernible among some tenants to prefer fixed produce contracts during the Boro/Rabi season, particularly in the agriculturally progressive areas. A crop-wise break-up of the lease-contracts reveals that, while the preponderance of share-crop tenancy has been almost exclusive for both categories of tenants in the case of the traditional crop, Aman paddy (cultivated during the Kharif season), tenancy has been changing its form, albeit at a slower rate, with the emergence of newer crops, such as Boro (summer) paddy, which is cultivated under improved technological conditions. There has also been a tendency towards the seasonalization of tenancy contracts. Thus, both categories of tenants endeavour to attract fresh tenancy contracts during tħe Boro/Rabi season which yields more flexibility towards functioning of a land-lease market during this season. As regards seasonal tenancy arrangements, the unrecorded tenants of lower size-groups obtain precedence.

The Changing Tenurial Relations

In order to bring into focus the changing aspect of tenurial relations following the organization and mobilization of the tenants under Operation Barga, we looked into the terms and conditions of tenancy contracts the two groups of tenants (unrecorded and recorded) have settled upon with their respective landlords. In this context, our study comes up with the following conclusions:

Crop-sharing: The recorded tenants, in spite of being accorded an extremely inferior socio-economic status vis-à-vis their lessors, are able to exercise their legal rights better in the matter of crop-sharing. This is contrary to the case with the unrecorded tenants, who are relatively more involved in the traditional equal-sharing of crop output with the lessors. This lends support to our hypothesis that the crop-sharing pattern has tended to become more favourable to the recorded tenants in the aftermath of their organized struggle in the state.

Cost-sharing: The incidence of cost-sharing has been ordinarily very low by the landlords of both categories of tenants. Although the landlords of the unrecorded tenants reveal a greater inclination towards sharing of some cost with them, yet the incidence of such cost-sharing cases has not been so great as to warrant the conclusion that recording of names by the tenants leads to non-participation in cost by the landlords. Another interesting aspect of cost-sharing is that when the landlords share in some input cost, they are invariably rewarded with a larger share of crop. In other words, cost-sharing acts as an instrument to eke out larger crop share for the landlord.

Factor market interlockings: Another important aspect of changing tenurial relations in West Bengal in recent years is that the transactions between the lessors and the lessees are being increasingly restricted to the land-lease market only. This has pushed the phenomenon of factor markets interlockings into insignificance. Thus, we observe no strong evidence of interlocking between land-lease and credit contracts. There is neither evidence of tenants being exploited by the landlords through a tie-up between tenancy and credit, nor any indication of credit being supplied by the landlords to improve the allocative efficiency of the tenants. All these developments suggest that most of the recently-developed theoretical models on tenancy-credit interlinking are rendered inapplicable in our study regions. There is, however, some evidence of interlinking between land-lease and labour contracts, particularly in agriculturally progressive areas and that, too, largely for a section of the unrecorded tenants. This interlinking operates mainly through the Boro season, whereby the tenants lease in land for Boro paddy cultivation and offer labour services for cultivation by the landlords on their self-operated portions of land. Nevertheless, what is more important is that the tenants do receive wages at the going market rate for such labour services, and tenancy-labour interlinking does not lead to any extra-economic coercion and the tenants do not lose their freedom to offer themselves in free wage labour market. In sum, the prevailing system does not appear to correspond to the feudal or semi-feudal relations so glibly enshrined in a large number of models on share-crop tenancy.

Non-recording by tenants: The seasonal nature of tenancy contracts and a desire to maintain good relation with the landlords appear as important reasons behind non-recording by a section of tenants. It is also possible that some tenants (unrecorded), while remaining outside the ambit of Kisan Sabha could not be mobilized to record their names. Nevertheless, there is no overwhelming evidence to suggest that the semi-feudal vested interests are obstructing them from recording their names in order to deprive the tenants of their tenancy rights. What appears more likely is that most such tenants voluntarily opted out from recording their names.

Tenants' access to credit: Compared with the unrecorded tenants, a relatively larger percentage of the recorded tenants are brought under the network of institutional credit agencies and a greater proportion of their credit requirement is met by the institutional credit agencies. However, in terms of availability of credit per loanee household from institutional agencies, they lag behind the unrecorded tenants slightly. Furthermore, the supply of institutional finance has not been adequate, so that quite a substantial section of the tenants are compelled to fall back upon non-institutional credit agencies. In so far as the non-institutional credit market functions rather imperfectly, there is indeed the need for greater policy intervention for breaking the nexus of non-institutional lenders, by strengthening the network of institutional credit agencies both in terms of covering a still larger section of recorded tenants and of supplying a greater quantum of credit to each borrowing household. Nevertheless, the prevailing situation does not provide forthright support to the view held in some circles that the recorded tenants have not been provided with alternative credit support which has become essential with the non-availability of credit from the landlords. The point we emphasize is that, to a great extent, even the unrecorded tenants do not depend on their landlords for credit support and the non-institutional credit market is very clearly dominated by non-landlord loan-givers.

Tenancy and Resource Allocation

The impact of tenancy on the allocation of resources and productivity level is brought out through the comparison of economic performances of the same set of households (owner-cum-tenants), between their owned and leased-in (sharecropped or fixed rented) plots of land. In this context, we observe a tendency among all categories of tenants (unrecorded and recorded) to apply a greater quantum of inputs per acre and gain a better productivity level on their owned land compared with their sharecropped portions of land. Thus, our study supports the theory of the misallocative function of crop-sharing tenancy vis-à-vis the sytem of ownership cultivation. No significant difference in economic performance is, however, discernible when a comparison is made between their owned and fixed-rent plots.

Operation Barga: Impact on Production?

What has the contribution of Operation Barga (O.B.) been in terms of actual gain in production is an important issue both for judging the economic rationale of such an important programme, as also to formulate a long-term policy for improving agricultural productivity and production. In so far as O.B. provided the recorded tenants the requisite bargaining power (by giving legal protection against eviction and rent-enhancement by the landlords) to correct the exploitative nature of tenancy and also to reset its terms and conditions in their favour, one would expect them to display better economic performance even on their sharecropped lands. However, contrary to such an expectation, we observe them practising a differential pattern as regards resource allocation between their owned and sharecropped lands even after recording. This, however, does not necessarily mean that the O.B. programme has dampened the growth of agricultural production for the following reasons:

(a) It is to be recognized that giving some legal protection to a tenant (as done through O.B.) on his leased-in land is really not equivalent to conferring upon him the right of ownership on the same land (which would have come through the implementation of the policy of 'land to the tiller'). This being so, there could still be the disincentive associated with the former so that the tenants might place their owned plots high in order of preference vis-à-vis sharecropped plots in the matter of allocation of resources even after recording. In other words, the recording of names of the tenants may not necessarily remove the total inefficiency of resource allocation (this is particularly true for the class of owner-cum-tenants) which flows from the very nature of crop-sharing arrangement, that is, where every gain in production owing to additional effort by the tenant automatically is shared with the landlord in the proportion contracted upon.

(b) Our main objection against the argument that O.B. produced a dampening effect on agricultural production flows from the comparison we make between the economic performances of the two groups of tenants on their owned/sharecropped lands. We observe that while the two groups of tenants do not differ much in terms of input utilization and productivity level on their owned plots, the recorded tenants tend to perform better, or at least competitively with the unrecorded tenants, as regards cultivation of sharecropped lands. We, therefore, maintain that O.B. has not resulted in any immediate loss of production, if it has not brought in dramatic gains of production.

Distribution of returns from crop production: It is also important that the usefulness or otherwise of a programme such as O.B. is to be judged not merely from its performance as a promoter of productive efficiency but also from its contribution towards setting more impartial distribution of returns from cultivation between the tenant and his landlord. On this latter count, O.B. deserves to be rated a success. This becomes clear when we compare the pattern of distribution of 'total returns' from cultivation for the two categories of tenants. Our data clearly show that the recorded tenants extract a much larger share of 'total returns' compared to the unrecorded tenants. This they do through a better exercise of their crop-sharing rights. Thus, through a better performing of its distributive function, O.B. leads to augmentation of income of a large section of recorded tenants.

Implication of the Prevailing Tenancy System for Agrarian Development

In the light of our discussion, one important issue that deserves some more clarification is: what is the implication of the prevailing tenancy system for agrarian development? In this context, the logical conclusion following from our study is that, with a vast majority of the tenants having successfully organized themselves to exert their tenancy rights and with tenancy assuming a more formal character replacing its traditional dependence-dominance format, the tenancy system as such should not be allowed to come in the way of agricultural development. Under the prevailing circumstances, if the tenants do not perform enough or even discriminate against their tenanted land vis-à-vis owned land in the matter of resource allocation, this is no more due to the exploitation of the feudal landlords (through usury, extracting 'begar' and so on) but because of the lack of ownership rights of the tenants on such lands. This may be termed as the 'pure disincentive effect' of tenant cultivation.

It is also to be remembered that with nearly one-eighth or slightly more of the cultivated area in the state being under tenant cultivation (as per 1982 N.S.S. estimates), it would be sheer exaggeration to put the entire blame for the lack of agricultural progress on the tenancy system. It needs to be underlined that the policies of agrarian reform being pursued in West Bengal, for instance, ensuring the tenancy rights of the tenants, distributing vested agricultural land to the landless/land-poor, breaking land concentration through the application of ceiling laws, are all directed towards creating a small-peasant oriented agrarian economy. To what extent such an economy will move towards higher growth paths would then depend largely upon the pace with which the vast majority of petty/small peasant farming units are turned into more productive and surplus-generating ones. The policies and programmes which could achieve this feat are subject to debate and discussion and hence we would like to leave the issue open. Nevertheless, a few points bear stressing:

First, a stage has perhaps come when, apart from pursuing the policies of institutional reform which help the perpetuation of small farming sector, it would now require a far greater degree of government intervention to make available a suitably devised package of technology along with adequate institutional finance to raise the performance of the small farming regime typical of West Bengal (and a number of other states in India). This is not to say that the course of institutional reform is complete in a state like West Bengal. With a section of the tenants as yet to be mobilized to record their names, the distribution of land-holdings still being far from equal and with the percentage of the landless households showing an increasing trend, not only does the case for pursuing the on-going scheme for institutional reform remain important, but there is also the need for a fresh review of the provisions and implementation of the existing reform legislation, particularly relating to the ceiling on land. However, we wish to emphasize that these should now follow concomitantly with more active government intervention for technological diffusion. The two most important areas where the government could assign priorities are the expansion of the irrigation network and the supply of institutional finance. Nearly three-fourths of the households operate less than 2.50 acres of land in West Bengal. The majority of them are presumably unable to make adequate irrigation arrangements of their own and the lack of irrigation alone could, sooner or later, whittle down further the growth of its petty/small peasant dominated agriculture. There is also a lot to be achieved in the sphere of expansion of institutional finance. Our own analysis clearly pinpoints the inadequacy of institutional finance even for the group of recorded sharecroppers who were to receive priority in this regard in recent years. We cannot lose sight of the fact that even now a fairly big percentage of tenants, recorded as well as unrecorded, do fall back upon non-institutional lenders and, consequently, suffer usurious extortions. Perhaps the steady expansion of the irrigation base, coupled with the provision of institutional finance, could bring about a dramatic transformation of small peasant dominated agrarian Bengal.

Second, it is time that the organizational spirit of the bulk of petty producers (including the sharecroppers) be channelized into achieving some degree of co-operation so as to reap the economies of scale for them. It is in this context that the leadership in panchayats could play an important role by encouraging the petty/small producers into forming co-operatives for undertaking overhead operations and investment, if not for going in for joint cultivation immediately. Let Schillerism be revived (Schiller, 1957).

Third, West Bengal with its ever-increasing burden of population on land is soon to exhaust the gains of its redistributive policy unless steps are taken to lessen the pressure of population on agricultural land. This is possible through industrializing both the rural and urban areas. Herein also lies a 'long-term solution' to the overall backwardness of West Bengal economy.

Relevance for Tenancy Reforms in Other Regions

Let us convey, in a few words, the message that the West Bengal experience has for tenancy reforms in many other states of India. It is well-known that, in many states of India, tenancy reforms have not made much headway owing to the long-drawn nature of the legislative process and the poor implementation of the provision of existing legislation. With the tenancy contracts being, by and large, oral, and with the lack of effective organization, the class of poor tenants has not been successful in withstanding the pressures from their landed patrons. In West Bengal, with the successful mobilization and organization of the tenants at the grass-roots level and with the genuine political will of the party in power to strike at rural vested interests, a vast majority of tenants could be provided with legal sanction for their tenancy right through the recording of their names. These recorded tenants are now more successful in the exercise of their tenancy rights and have been able to challenge the age-old exploitative character of tenancy relationships, mainly on the basis of their organizational strength. The West Bengal experience recommends the case for launching a vigorous mobilization and organization of the mass of poor tenants in collaboration with other weaker sections at the grass-roots level. It is a fact that such mobilization and organization in West Bengal came after a historical chain of events (several peasant uprisings during the colonial period, the tebhaga movement at the dawn of Independence and the Naxalite movement since the mid-sixties), but their organizational base has been strengthened only in recent years with the revival of the Panchayati Raj system. In the event of organizational weaknesses of the rural poor in many regions of India, the revival of Panchayati Raj system may be contemplated as a first step towards the launching the process of political mobilization at the grass-roots level. The need of the hour is to raise the degree of political consciousness of the weaker sections through their direct involvement in the local-level planning and administration. If the governments in power at the centre and other states are sincere about improving the lot of the rural poor (including the petty tenant cultivators), the West Bengal experience has a clear message for them.

A final point on the usefulness of land reform measures (of

which tenancy reform is a part) may be made in the context of economic policy changes recently initiated by the government at the centre. It is to be noted that, as in the past, the programme of land reforms does not find a concrete place in the agenda of the government. At the present moment, the government seems to be heading for a non-subsidized strategy of agricultural development while laying greater stress on building a modern industrial sector through a policy of 'liberalization and privatization'. In its policy of industrialization, the government also appears to be depending more on 'external markets'. The appropriateness of such a strategy of economic development forms a subject which does not strictly fall within the purview of the present study. Nevertheless, we would like to emphasize that land reform programmes, if implemented seriously, could contribute to the very process of industrialization. Under the regime of successful implementation of land reform measures, the industrialization programme benefits through the augmentation of incomes of the mass of rural poor which, in turn, generates the 'internal market' for industrial output. It also helps establish a self-reliant industrial structure. This apart, the strengthening of rural institutions, including land reform institutions, remains important under all epochs, for the sake of achieving the efficient functioning of markets as also for the welfare of the majority of the rural people. We are thus in broad agreement with the consensus at a recent seminar that 'an effective implementation of land reforms could contribute to efficient functioning of markets and to a non-subsidised agricultural growth, while simultaneously contributing to the goals of improved employment and equity' (see Haque and Parthasarathy, 1992: 397).

Appendices

APPENDIX I: SELECTION OF SAMPLE AREA AND THE MODE OF PRIMARY DATA COLLECTION

For the sake of examining various issues relating to tenancy in Bengal, our choice of the district of Midnapore is deliberate. We are aware that no sweeping generalization on tenancy for the state as a whole on the basis of the experience of a single district would be advisable. However, the fact remains that data collected from a given region may be useful even to test some of the broader issues relating to the institution, such as tenancy and changing tenurial relations provided the chosen district comes, as far as possible, nearer to the average position for the state as a whole.

The district of Midnapore has been predominantly rural, with nearly 91 per cent of its population living in rural areas in 1981. In recent years, Midnapore has undergone some changes in the structure of its agriculture. Most notable in this context is changes in cropping pattern with the penetration of modern biological inputs. As is true for the state of West Bengal as a whole, a notable feature of the changing cropping pattern has been the emergence of Boro paddy as an important crop. The increase in the proportion of cropped area under commercial crops such as potatoes and vegetables have also been commendable (see Appendix Table A7).

The available data on agricultural inputs and technology show that in 1984–85, nearly 16 per cent of gross cropped area in the district was irrigated by canals which is slightly higher than the average figure for West Bengal (Appendix Table A8). In recent years, the district also benefited from public investment in irrigation. As on March 1986, nearly 11 per cent of river lift irrigation schemes, 7 per cent of deep tubewells and 6 per cent of the state-owned shallow tubewells of the state are located in Midnapore alone.[1] It is true that in terms of irrigated cropped area (taken for five crops, namely, Aman paddy, Aus paddy, Boro paddy, wheat and jute) and per cropped hectare consumption of fertilizer, the district occupies a position slightly lower than the average for the state. However, in terms of

---

[1] The data on irrigation installations are supplied by the Directorate of Agricultural Engineering, Government of West Bengal.

yield rate of rice, the most important crop of the state, the district does not differ much from the state.

As regards the land tenure system, Midnapore is known to have occupied, during the pre-Independence period, an intermediate position between the temporarily settled provinces of Orissa and the permanently settled districts of Bengal proper and, accordingly, is some type of an amalgam of both the systems (Hunter, 1876: 100). In the permanently settled parts, three different tenures existed (*ibid.*: 86–96): (*a*) ordinary rent-paying tenures; (*b*) rent-free tenures; and (*c*) rent-free service tenures. Under the second type, the tenures consisted of *debottar lands, brahmottar lands* and so on while, under the third, lands were granted free of rent in return for military or other services performed by the grantee. The ordinary rent-paying tenures consisted of twenty-five different tenures (*ibid.*: 90–91)— *zamindaris, taluks, patnis, izaras* and so on. The under-tenures below the rank of zamindar usually spread up to the third degree in Midnapore following the hierarchy *zamindar-patnidar-darpatnidar-sepatnis.* The zamindars also used to have *nij jot, khamar* or *sir lands* which they cultivated either by hired labour or by tenants-at-will, that is, the bargadars. Further, the reclamation of waste lands in some areas led to the creation of *bhag jot* (sharecropped) tenures whereby the tiller cultivated the land with his own plough, bore all expenses of cultivation and retained half of the gross produce as his share handing over the other half to the landlord or his superior tenant, as the case may be.

It is not possible to fix one single estimate either of the percentage of bargadars among rural households or the percentage of area under barga cultivation in Midnapore during the pre-Independence period. While the Survey and Settlement Report for Midnapore (1911–17) recorded 6.4 per cent of net cropped area as barga land, the estimate provided by the McAlpin Report (1914) shows 52 per cent of under-ryotee land under barga cultivation (Chaudhuri, 1975c: 156). The Report of the Land Revenue Commission (1940) reported that 6.5 per cent of the agricultural families in Midnapore acted mainly/entirely as bargadars while the proportion of land cultivated by them was estimated to be 17.1 per cent. The Report also admitted that such figures might provide underestimates because *sanja* tenants and *utbandi* tenants (those were fixed-rent tenancies) were not included in the definition of bargadars.

As regards the extent of tenant cultivation in Midnapore for the post-Independence period, the 1951 Census data reveal that 19 per cent of agricultural land in Midnapore is cultivated by the bargadars (Census of India, 1951: 481). The 1961 Census reported 32 per cent of cultivating households having interest in land as bargadars (Census of India, 1961: 108). This latter report also noted that the percentage of bargadars is higher among the tribal cultivating households. About 44 per cent of tribal agricultural families are reported as bargadars in 1961. The National

Sample Survey Report for 1971–72 (26th Round) shows that in the western region of West Bengal comprising the districts of Bankura, Midnapore and Purulia, nearly 13 per cent of operated area represented the tenanted land of which nearly 89 per cent was cultivated on crop-sharing basis.[2] In a recent survey conducted in 1981–82, the percentage of barga land in the zone comprising the districts of Midnapore and 24–Parganas is estimated to be 7.30 per cent of owned area (see Bandyopadhyay *et al.*, 1983: 28). Although data drawn from various sources are not strictly comparable, what appears from these diverse estimates is that the extent of tenant cultivation is on the decline in the district, in conformity with the general trend observed earlier for the state as a whole.(Chapter II). Nevertheless, a significant proportion of area can still be found under tenant cultivation particularly in some specific areas of the district.

An important aspect of tenant cultivation in Midnapore is that a vast majority of the tenants have recorded their names following their political mobilization in recent years. According to official estimates, the number of bargadars recorded till the end of 1984 show that out of 1.31 million bargadars recorded in West Bengal, the share of Midnapore alone is nearly 22 per cent (Ghosh, 1986).

The sample blocks: Since the district is administratively divided into two parts, Midnapore (East) and Midnapore (West), we thought it advisable to choose two blocks from each—one relatively 'advanced' and the other relatively 'backward'. Since our emphasis is on the issue of agricultural tenancy it is very essential that the chosen blocks have a sufficiently big concentration of tenants, both recorded and unrecorded. After detailed inquiries and investigation, we chose Daspur I and Daspur II in Midnapore (East) and Debra and Sankrail in Midnapore (West).

The two blocks chosen from Midnapore (East), being contiguous to each other, represent fairly homogeneous agro-climatic conditions. However, in terms of irrigation infrastructure, Daspur I is much better placed than Daspur II. Similarly, among the blocks in Midnapore (West), while Debra gets irrigation largely from government-owned deep-tubewells, Sankrail is deficient in irrigation and fall in the backward dry region of the western part of the district.

To answer our requirement, the sample blocks have a fairly good concentration of tenancy. While the two blocks in Midnapore (West) have a greater concentration of recorded tenants, those in Midnapore (East) have a higher concentration of unrecorded tenants. Moreover, the two blocks in Midnapore (West) have a higher concentration of tribal population, many of whom work as agricultural labourer-cum-sharecroppers.

---

[2] National Sample Survey Organisation, *Tables on Land Holdings*, 26th Round (July 1971–September 1972), Report No. 215.21, Vol. II, p. 172.

Furthermore, these areas witnessed a violent outburst of peasant uprisings during the Naxalite period of the late sixties/early seventies (see Dasgupta, 1973; Maity, 1978).

The sample villages: We decided to cover three villages from each block. Here again, one precondition was that the sample villages should correspond to the overall features of the blocks and should have a fair concentration of sharecroppers, if possible both recorded and unrecorded. It was also essential that we establish some rapport with panchayat members/officials and other respected and knowledgeable persons in the villages who could be mobilized in order to persuade the tenant households to respond to our queries. Such a rapport is a *sine qua non* in ensuring the reliability of sample information for a study of a very sensitive nature, such as this one.

Appendix Table A9 provides the list of villages in each block along with a brief profile of some of their characteristic features. It emerges that in terms of availability of irrigation facilities and cropping pattern, the villages in Daspur I and Debra represent the most progressive agricultural pockets of the district. These villages are thus put together and designated as a relatively advanced Region I. On the other hand, as the villages in Daspur II and Sankrail represent relatively backward areas, they are considered together to constitute the lagging Region II.

The conduct of field survey: In our field survey, while we covered almost all the lessee households in each village, a major difficulty was encountered with respect to the lessor households. Among the lessors, those with non-agricultural activities as primary occupation, would usually reside outside the village for most of the year and were therefore not accessible. As regards those residing within the village, our preliminary investigations led us to believe that tactically it may not have been advisable to approach them with our questionnaire.[3] Instead, an alternative device was to ask lessees for information about their lessors. The information so obtained is broadly verified from other persons in the village. Operationally, this became easier in the cases where more than one tenant leased in from a common lessor.

The fieldwork was conducted in three stages. In the first stage, we tried to meet members of the sample households individually so as to acquaint them with the purpose of the study and to assure them that the information to be gathered had nothing to do with the government machinery and would in no circumstances be utilized against their interest. This visit also helped us a great deal in acquainting ourselves with the village economy.

[3] It may be noted in this connection that some other researchers on the subject of tenancy also preferred to exclude the category of lessors from their sample on consideration of reliability of information. See for example, Bardhan and Rudra (1980).

For actual data collection, a comprehensive questionnaire was prepared and duly pre-tested in one of the sample villages. The final questionnaire was canvassed at all households. The second stage of the survey continued between November 1986 and February 1987 covering the Kharif season. The final visit ranged between May 1987 and July 1987 and covered the Rabi/Boro season. It was during the final visit, by which time we could further consolidate our rapport with the tenants, that we put the more sensitive questions relating to terms and conditions of tenancy contracts to our respondents.

The reference period for field survey in this study is the agricultural year July 1986 to June 1987.

APPENDIX II: DEFINITIONS

Lessor/Landlord: A person who leases out his land at least in one of the agricultural seasons.

Lessee/Tenant: A person who leases in some land, at least in one of the two seasons. The person may also lease out a fraction of his land during any particular part of the year, but the net area leased in (area leased in minus area leased out) is positive. There are two categories of lessees in our sample—recorded and unrecorded. The recorded lessees have registered their names under the programme of Operation Barga or even before the launching of this programme. These tenants enjoy legal protection against rent-enhancement and eviction by the landowners. They also get some other benefits devised for them in recent years. The unrecorded tenants have not gone in for recording their names and are reflective of the traditional form of tenancy arrangement. They are liable to eviction at the discretion of the landowners.

Owned Land: It consists of all lands (cultivable and uncultivable) under the heritable possession of the household. Here, heritable possession is tantamount to what is generally known as occupancy right. The household may have heritable possession over a piece of land with or without the right to sell such the same. Thus the land given to the landless, near-landless and marginal farmers (under the scheme of redistribution of vested lands) is to be included under the category of owned land.

Owned Cultivated Land: It represents area owned minus uncultivable land (which includes homestead, pond, orchards and so on) and current fallow plus net mortgaged area.

Leased in Land: Leased in land represents the area leased in by a tenant under any form of contract. For example, land leased in by a recorded/unrecorded tenant may be under crop-sharing or fixed rent (kind/cash) contract.

Operational Land: This includes all parcels of land falling within the scope of distinct management for cultivation by the household. It is defined as owned cultivated land plus net leased in area. In this study, operational area by a household is calculated separately for the Kharif and the Rabi/Boro seasons.

Human Labour Days: Labour days actually spent on crop production by family members of the household, permanent labour and casual labour. The family component actually consists of labour put in by adult males, adult females and by children (below the age of 14 years in our study). In order to standardize these heterogeneous elements, we have standardized family labour days by considering the difference in market wage rate for these categories. As regards the wage rate between male and female casual labourers, no great difference exists in our study area except for the weeding operation (mostly in jute). Child labour gets a lower wage than an adult male/female labour and the ratio between the two is used for finding standardized labour days put in by children in a family. Permanent labour is of no great use in our study area. It is used occasionally for the purpose of ploughing. Whenever it is used, we simply inquired the days put in by the permanent labour. Casual labour is mostly hired to perform major operations such as sowing and harvesting. The wage-bill for casual labour is calculated by considering the wage rate prevailing in village labour market for different seasons.

Bullock Labour Days: The number of days spent by a pair of bullocks on field crop operations. The cost of hired-in bullock labour is evaluated at the going market rate.

Material Inputs: Include cost incurred on seeds, manures, fertilizers, insecticides and pesticides. Seeds and manures may be home produced or purchased. The value of home produced seeds and manures are evaluated at market price prevailing locally in the village. Fertilizers and insecticides and pesticides are of diverse types and quality so that each one of them is evaluated separately at the purchase price and added together to obtain total expenditure on them. The value of all material inputs comprise total cost on material inputs.

Other Inputs: It shows all costs on such items as irrigation, hiring in of agricultural implements and so on. In case of own irrigation, the cost of running the irrigation equipment is considered. For purchased irrigation, the actual price paid by the household is taken into consideration. Similarly, costs of hiring in of other agricultural implements (such as, paddle threshers, sprayers, bullock carts) are included in the category of other inputs.

Output: The value of farm produce including the value of by-products. It is calculated for each crop separately. In order to express it in value terms, the physical quantity (main crop and its by-product) is multiplied by the harvest price in the nearby village market.

APPENDIX TABLE A1: *Land-use Pattern in West Bengal*

Item	Three-year average centred in					
	1951–52	1960–61	1970–71	1980–81	1985–86
(a) Net Sown Area ('000 hectare)	4803	5421	5491	5499	5443
(b) Index (1970–73 = 100)	87.47	98.73	100.00	100.15	99.13
Percentage of Net Sown Area to Cultivable Area	91.49	93.21	94.36	98.02	98.83
Land-man Ratio (in acre)	0.63	0.50	0.41	0.34	0.31
(a) Gross Sown Area ('000 hectare)	5484	6355	7177	7061	7356
(b) Index (1970–73 = 100)	76.41	88.51	100.00	98.38	102.49
Cropping Intensity	1.14	1.17	1.31	1.28	1.35

Source: (a) Statistical Abstract, West Bengal (various years);
(b) Bureau of Applied Economics and Statistics, West Bengal.

Note: Cultivable area means 'net sown area plus current fallow; Land-man ratio = Net sown area: rural population.

APPENDIX TABLE A2: *Cropping Pattern in West Bengal (Percentage to Gross Cropped Area)*

Crop	Three-year average centred in:					
	1951–52	1960–61	1970–71	1980–81	1985–86
Rice (Aus)	8.98	9.22	11.13	9.15	7.93
Rice (Aman)	63.24	60.77	55.61	58.80	55.45
Rice (Boro)	0.33	0.54	2.77	4.24	7.53
Rice (total)	72.55	70.53	69.51	72.19	70.91
Wheat	0.89	0.68	4.59	4.75	4.71
Cereals (total)	75.09	73.25	76.06	78.49	77.09
Gram	2.98	2.82	2.10	1.25	0.92
Pulses (total)	11.60	11.94	9.16	7.19	5.33
Foodgrains (total)	86.69	85.20	85.22	85.69	84.41
Rape and mustard	1.64	1.65	1.48	1.94	3.50
Oilseeds (total)	2.23	2.53	2.35	4.24	5.36
Sugarcane	0.37	0.56	0.52	0.31	0.18
Jute	5.78	5.71	6.06	7.69	8.08
Potato	0.74	0.92	0.92	1.62	2.08

Sources: As in Appendix Table A1.

APPENDIX TABLE A3: *Rates of Growth of Area (A), Yield (Y) and Production (P) of Major Crops in West Bengal*

Crop	1957–58 to 1966–67			1967–68 to 1976–77			1977–78 to 1986–87			1957–58 to 1986–87		
	A	Y	P	A	Y	P	A	Y	P	A	Y	P
Rice (Aus)	0.64	0.90	1.53	0.56	-0.14	0.42	-1.13	1.29	0.17	0.10	0.33	0.41
Rice (Aman)	0.30	0.54	1.07	0.31	0.29	0.03	0.06	0.56	0.62	0.23	0.44	0.67
Rice (Boro)	0.68	1.84	2.44	7.67	0.75	8.45	3.30	0.13	3.43	5.62	1.79	7.41
Rice (total)	0.35	0.57	1.12	0.59	0.06	0.66	0.18	0.86	1.04	0.29	0.53	0.80
Wheat	1.56	0.99	2.52	7.97	1.50	9.48	-1.81	0.93	-0.89	4.29	2.19	6.45
Cereals (total)	0.34	0.58	0.91	0.92	0.32	1.24	0.03	0.85	0.88	0.40	0.62	1.02
Gram	-0.63	1.39	0.75	-3.57	0.51	-3.03	-2.22	0.59	-1.63	-1.74	0.59	-1.14
Pulses (total)	0.85	0.85	1.70	-0.57	0.13	-0.30	-2.23	0.79	-1.45	-1.01	0.28	-0.72
Foodgrains (total)	0.40	0.57	0.96	0.76	0.39	1.15	-0.14	0.95	0.81	0.26	0.68	0.94
Rape and mustard	0.50	0.63	1.08	-1.39	-0.08	-1.37	5.27	0.10	7.31	1.16	0.67	2.06
Oilseeds (total)	0.82	0.83	1.62	0.51	0.01	0.50	3.18	2.17	5.33	1.65	0.93	2.56
Sugarcane	1.27	0.56	1.91	-0.42	0.83	0.36	-4.20	0.01	-4.37	-1.00	0.53	-0.51
Jute	1.73	0.08	1.82	-0.12	1.02	0.88	0.57	1.39	1.97	0.68	0.46	1.14
Potato	2.26	0.18	2.50	2.38	3.05	4.46	1.06	1.53	2.67	1.65	1.31	2.98

Note: Estimating equation for growth rate: ln Q = a + bt and growth rate = b × 100.

APPENDIX TABLE A4: *Some Indicators of Expansion of Agricultural Inputs and Technology in West Bengal*

Item	1960–61	1970–71	1980–81	1985–86
Percentage of net irrigated area to net sown area	25.77	–	27.03	34.25*
Percentage of gross irrigated area to gross sown area	22.30	23.06	20.98	–
Crops irrigated (percentage of area):				
Aus Paddy	–	–	9.24	14.79
Aman Paddy	–	–	22.27	24.21
Boro Paddy	–	–	86.64	95.00
Total Paddy	27.38	–	25.20	30.87
Wheat	64.57	–	80.07	88.65
Jute	–	–	12.39	21.37
HYV area (percentage):				
Aus Paddy	–	8.89**	35.75	37.88
Aman Paddy	–	10.12**	22.91	31.98
Boro Paddy	–	84.67***	100.00	99.94
Total Paddy	–	14.46**	29.60	39.40
Wheat	–	91.21**	100.00	100.00
Fertilizer consumption per hectare of gross sown area	2.38	13.60	38.51	55.57
No. per thousand hectare of gross sown area				
Plough (iron & wooden)	338	182	182***	–
Sugarcane crusher	0.84	0.11	–	–
Irr. pumps (diesel and others)	0.61	0.99	–	–
Tractors	0.05	0.08	–	–
Percentage of villages electrified	–	7.76	37.51	54.00
No. of regulated markets per million of rural population	–	2.10	7.70	7.40
Percentage of advances to deposits of commercial banks in rural areas	–	35.05†	30.53††	39.92‡

Sources: *Statistical Abstract, West Bengal* (various years); *Economic Review, West Bengal* (various years); *Statistical Abstract, India* (various years); *Agricultural Productivity in Eastern India*, Vol. II, Reserve Bank of India, 1984; Bureau of Applied Economics and Statistics, West Bengal.

Notes: * relates to 1982–83; ** relates to 1971–72; *** relates to 1977; † relates to June 1978; †† relates to June 1982; ‡ relates to September 1986.

APPENDIX TABLE A5: *Educational Status of Tenant Households*

Item	Unrecorded tenants:		Recorded tenants:		All tenants:	
	Region I	Region II	Region I	Region II	Region I	Region II
Percentage of male members with education level:						
Primary	44.76	48.11	38.14	45.63	41.83	46.96
Middle	40.48	31.89	39.18	30.00	39.85	31.01
Matric	4.29	3.78	2.58	1.25	3.47	2.61
Up to Graduate	0.95	0.54	2.06	1.25	1.49	0.87
Percentage of male literates	90.48	84.32	81.96	78.13	86.64	81.45
Percentage of male illiterates	9.52	15.68	18.04	21.87	13.36	18.55
Percentage of female members with education level:						
Primary	30.94	34.91	16.86	29.71	24.08	32.57
Middle	18.23	16.57	18.02	14.49	18.13	15.64
Matric	–	–	–	–	–	–
Up to Graduate	–	–	–	–	–	–
Percentage of female literates	49.17	51.48	34.88	44.20	42.21	48.21
Percentage of female illiterates	50.83	48.52	65.22	55.80	57.79	51.79

Note: For calculating the percentage of households with different education levels, members with 6+ age alone are considered.

APPENDIX TABLE A6: *Crop-wise Distribution of Lease Contracts Under Crop-sharing and Fixed-rent Tenancies by Region and Size-class of Tenant Operational Holdings (Number of Cases)*

Region	Crop	Contractual form	Size of operational holding of tenants (in acres):									
			Unrecorded					Recorded				
			Less than 1.00	1.00 to 2.49	2.50 to 4.99	5.00 & above	Total	Less than 1.00	1.00 to 2.49	2.50 to 4.99	5.00 & above	Total
I	Aman paddy	Crop-sharing	10	12	12	2	36	9	22	8	2	41
		Fixed-rent	–	–	1	–	1	1	5	1	–	7
		Total	10	12	13	2	37	10	27	9	2	48
II	Aman paddy	Crop-sharing	16	22	4	2	44	24	11	4	–	39
		Fixed-rent	–	–	–	–	–	–	–	–	–	–
		Total	16	22	4	2	44	24	11	4	–	39
I	Boro paddy	Crop-sharing	16	16	12	1	45	10	19	9	2	40
		Fixed-rent	14	5	7	–	26	1	4	1	–	6
		Total	30	21	19	1	71	11	23	10	2	46
II	Boro paddy	Crop-sharing	26	22	2	1	51	12	4	–	–	16
		Fixed-rent	1	1	1	–	3	–	–	–	–	–
		Total	27	23	3	1	54	12	4	–	–	16
I	Jute	Crop-sharing	7	3	3	1	14	–	3	1	–	4
		Fixed-rent	–	–	1	–	1	–	1	–	–	1
		Total	7	3	4	1	15	–	4	1	–	5
II	Jute	Crop-sharing	4	9	1	1	15	2	3	2	–	7
		Fixed-rent	–	–	–	–	–	–	–	–	–	–
		Total	4	9	1	1	15	2	3	2	–	7

Appendix Table A6 (Contd.)

Region	Crop	Contractual form	Size of operational holding of tenants (in acres):									
			Unrecorded					Recorded				
			Less than 1.00	1.00 to 2.49	2.50 to 4.99	5.00 & above	Total	Less than 1.00	1.00 to 2.49	2.50 to 4.99	5.00 & above	Total
II	Aus paddy	Crop-sharing	2	–	–	–	3	–	4	–	–	4
		Fixed-rent	–	–	–	–	–	–	–	–	–	–
		Total	2	–	–	–	3	–	4	–	–	4
II	Sugarcane	Crop-sharing	4	2	2	1	9	3	5	1	–	9
		Fixed-rent	1	–	–	–	1	2	–	–	–	2
		Total	5	2	2	1	10	5	5	1	–	11
I	Potato	Crop-sharing	6	3	5	2	16	1	2	–	–	3
		Fixed-rent	–	1	–	–	1	–	1	–	–	1
		Total	6	4	5	2	17	1	3	–	–	4
II	Potato	Crop-sharing	3	2	–	1	6	–	–	–	–	–
		Fixed-rent	–	1	–	–	1	–	–	–	–	–
		Total	3	3	–	1	7	–	–	–	–	–
I	Karala	Crop-sharing	1	–	–	–	1	–	–	–	–	–
		Fixed-rent	–	3	3	–	6	–	1	–	–	1
		Total	1	3	3	–	7	–	1	–	–	1
II	Karala	Crop-sharing	1	–	–	–	1	–	–	–	–	–
		Fixed-rent	1	–	–	–	–	–	–	–	–	–
		Total	1	–	–	–	1	–	–	–	–	–

APPENDIX TABLE A7: *Cropping Pattern in Midnapore District*

Year	Aman paddy	Aus paddy	Boro paddy	Total paddy	Wheat	Pulses	Total food-grains	Oil-seeds	Jute	Sugar-cane	Potato	Vege-tables
							Proportion of cropped area under:					
1960–61	78.71	5.92	0.90	85.53	0.01	8.92	95.02	0.50	0.84	0.10	0.56	NA
1965–66	78.49	4.13	0.32	82.95	0.02	9.72	93.27	0.66	1.34	0.25	1.06	NA
1970–71	74.29	7.21	5.23	86.74	0.96	5.72	93.67	0.58	1.13	0.35	0.95	NA
1975–76	74.91	4.50	6.56	85.97	2.81	6.62	95.70	0.94	1.07	0.28	1.35	NA
1984–85	70.77	4.45	8.13	83.36	1.22	3.21	87.79	2.74	1.06	0.10	2.47	2.71

Source: Annual Plan on Agriculture 1985–86, Midnapore (East) and Midnapore (West).
Note: NA = Not available.

APPENDIX TABLE A8: *Some Indicators of Levels of Agricultural Technology in the Districts of West Bengal*

District	Yield of rice (Kgs./Ha) (1985–86)	Fertilizer consumption (Kgs./Ha) (1985–86)	Proportion of gross cropped area irrigated by canals (1984–85)	Percentage of cropped area irrigated* (1985–86)
Burdwan	1880	83.5	44.2	70.0
Birbhum	1722	59.2	41.2	69.6
Bankura	1788	43.1	40.8	56.4
Midnapore	1576	41.1	15.9	23.1
Hoogly	1976	150.5	28.3	52.3
Purulia	1756	34.9	7.3	17.8
24-Parganas	1380	55.2	–	15.4
Howrah	1831	153.9	4.4	26.1
Nadia	2052	56.2	–	55.6
Murshidabad	1583	51.2	8.1	49.9
West Dinajpur	1234	31.3	–	9.6
Malda	1642	67.9	–	26.3
Jalpaiguri	1028	19.5	1.4	0.5
Darjeeling**	1187	55.8	1.7	37.3
Cooch Behar	1043	35.2	0.1	1.4
West Bengal***	1573	55.6	13.6	31.6

Sources: 1. Economic Review for West Bengal, 1987–88.
2. Bureau of Applied Economics and Statistics, West Bengal.
Notes: * Includes five crops, namely, Aman paddy, Aus paddy, Boro paddy, wheat and jute;
** Siliguri sub-division only;
*** Excluding hilly sub-divisions of Darjeeling district.

APPENDIX TABLE A9: *Brief Profile of the Sample Villages*

Block	Village	Population (1981)	Scheduled castes (%)	Scheduled tribes (%)	Cultivators (%)	Agril. labourers (%)	Principal source of irrigation	Principal crops
Daspur I	Rajnagar	3,319	47.03	–	70.36	18.08	STW, Canal & Pumpset	Aman paddy, Boro paddy, jute, potato & vegetables
	Kalara	1,506	15.80	0.86	63.13	18.95	RLI, DTW, Canal & Pumpset	Aman paddy, Boro paddy, jute, potato & vegetables
	Khar Radha-krishnapur	848	33.61	1.65	46.65	20.70	Canal & Pumpset	Aman paddy, Boro paddy, jute, potato & vegetables
Debra	Benya	907	6.28	3.42	70.64	24.13	DTW & Canal	Aman paddy & Boro paddy
	Abdalipore	1,034	26.02	38.97	66.34	16.14	DTW & Canal	Aman paddy & Boro paddy
	Brindabanchak-Hadira	661	5.45	18.61	77.78	20.74	STW	Aman paddy & Boro paddy
Daspur II	Sahachak	1,417	12.56	–	71.15	19.07	STW & Canal	Aman paddy & jute
	Kelegoda	1,829	30.12	–	44.74	23.71	STW	Aman paddy, Boro paddy & jute

Appendix Table A9 (Contd.)

Block	Village	Population (1981)	Scheduled castes (%)	Scheduled tribes (%)	Cultivators (%)	Agril. labourers (%)	Principal source of irrigation	Principal crops
	Rana	1,154	10.49	–	55.28	17.59	STW	Aman paddy, Boro paddy & jute
Sankrail	Baharadari	974	24.05	–	45.99	33.58	STW & Pumpset	Aman paddy, Aus paddy & sugarcane
	Sripur	427	34.89	15.93	10.30	61.21	STW & Pumpset	Aman paddy & sugarcane
	Harekrishnapur	454	56.61	7.05	36.76	58.09	RLI	Aman paddy, Boro paddy & sugarcane

Sources: Census of India, 1981; District Census Handbook, Midnapore; Field Survey.
Notes: DTW = Deep Tubewell; STW = Shallow Tubewell; and RLI = River Lift Irrigation.

APPENDIX TABLE A10: *Distribution of Households over Sample Blocks*

Block	Number of tenants		
	Unrecorded	Recorded	Total
Daspur I	45	22	67
Debra	19	34	53
Daspur II	49	21	70
Sankrail	8	26	34
Total	121	103	224

References

ADAMS, D.W. and N. RASK. (1968), 'Economics of Cost-Share Leases in Less Developed Countries', *American Journal of Agricultural Economics*, Vol. 50, November.

ATHREYA, VENKATESH et al. (1987), 'Identification of Agrarian Classes: A Methodological Essay with Empirical Material from South India', *Journal of Peasant Studies*, Vol. 14, No. 2, January.

BAGCHI, AMIYA KUMAR. (1973), 'Some Implications of Unemployment in Rural Areas', *Economic and Political Weekly*, Vol. 3, Special Number, August.

——————. (1975), 'Cropsharing Tenancy in Agriculture: A Rejoinder', *Economic and Political Weekly*, Vol. 10, No. 30, 26 July.

——————. (1976), 'Cropsharing Tenancy and Neoclassical Economics', *Economic and Political Weekly*, Vol. 11, No. 3, 17 January.

——————. (1982), *The Political Economy of Underdevelopment*, Cambridge University Press, Cambridge.

BAGI, F.S. (1981), 'Economics of Share-Cropping in Haryana (India) Agriculture', *Pakistan Development Review*, Vol. 20, No. 1.

BANDYOPADHYAY, D. (1980), *Land Reforms in West Bengal*, Government of West Bengal, June.

——————. (1986), 'Land Reforms in India: An Analysis', *Economic and Political Weekly*, Vol. 21, Nos. 25–26, 21–28 June.

BANDYOPADHYAY, NRIPEN. (1975), 'Changing Forms of Agricultural Enterprise in West Bengal', *Economic and Political Weekly*, Vol. 10, No. 17, 26 April.

——————. (1975), 'Land Reform and Sharecropping', *Mainstream*, 17 May.

——————. (1977), 'Causes of Sharp Increase in Agricultural Labourers, 1961–71: A Study of Social Existence Forms of Labour in North Bengal', *Economic and Political Weekly*, Vol. 12, No. 53, 31 December.

——————. (1980), 'Santal Insurrection to Operation Barga', in *From Santal Insurrection to Operation Barga* (in Bengali), Government of West Bengal, Board of Revenue, October.

——————. (1981), 'Operation Barga and Land Reforms Perspective in West Bengal: A Discursive Review', *Economic and Political Weekly*, Vol. 16, Nos. 25–26, 20–27 June.

——————. (1988), 'The Story of Land Reforms in Indian Planning', in Amiya Kumar Bagchi (ed.), *Economy, Society and Politics: Essays in the Political Economy of Indian Planning*, Oxford University Press, Delhi.

BANDYOPADHYAY, NRIPEN AND ASSOCIATES. (1983), *Evaluation of Land Reforms Measures in West Bengal: A Report*, Centre for Studies in Social Sciences, Calcutta.

BARDHAN, PRANAB K. (1976), 'Variations in Extent and Forms of Agricultural Tenancy-II', *Economic and Political Weekly*, Vol. 11, No. 38, 18 September.

—————. (1980), 'Interlocking Factor Markets and Agrarian Development: A Review of Issues', *Oxford Economic Papers*, Vol. 32, No. 1.

—————. (1984), *Land, Labour and Rural Poverty: Essays in Development Economics*, Oxford University Press, Delhi.

BARDHAN, PRANAB K. and ASHOK RUDRA. (1978), 'Interlinkage of Land Labour and Credit Relations: An Analysis of Village Survey Data in East India', *Economic and Political Weekly*, Vol. 13, Nos. 6–7, February.

—————. (1980), 'Terms and Conditions of Sharecropping Contracts: An Analysis of Village Survey Data in India', *Journal of Development Studies*, Vol. 16, No. 3, April.

BARDHAN, P.K. and T.N. SRINIVASAN. (1971), 'Cropsharing Tenancy in Agriculture: A Theoretical and Empirical Analysis', *American Economic Review*, Vol. 41, No. 1.

—————. (1974), 'Cropsharing Tenancy in Agriculture: Rejoinder', *American Economic Review*, Vol. 64, December.

BASU, KAUSHIK. (1984), *The Less Developed Economy: A Critique of Contemporary Theory*, Oxford University Press, Delhi.

BELL, CLIVE. (1977), 'Alternative Theories of Sharecropping: Some Tests Using Evidence from Northeast India', *Journal of Development Studies*, Vol. 13, No. 4.

—————. (1986), 'The Choice of Tenancy Contracts', paper presented at the *Eighth World Congress of the International Economic Association*, New Delhi, December 4.

—————. (1991), 'Markets, Power and Productivity in Rural Asia: A Review Article', *Journal of Development Economics*, Vol. 36, No. 2, October.

BELL, CLIVE and T.N. SRINIVASAN. (1989), 'Integrated Transactions in Rural Markets: An Empirical Study of Andhra Pradesh, Bihar and Punjab', *Oxford Bulletin of Economics and Statistics*, Vol. 51, No. 1.

BETTELHEIM, CHARLES. (1977), *India Independent*, Khosla and Co., Delhi.

BHADURI, AMIT. (1973), 'A Study of Agricultural Backwardness Under Semi-Feudalism', *Economic Journal*, Vol. 83, March.

—————. (1983), *The Economic Structure of Backward Agriculture*, Macmillan, London.

—————. (1986), 'Forced Commerce and Agrarian Growth', *World Development*, Vol. 14, No. 2.

BHADURI, AMIT et al. (1986), 'Persistence and Polarisation: A Study in the Dynamics of Agrarian Contradiction', *Journal of Peasant Studies*, Vol. 13, No. 3, April.

BHARADWAJ, KRISHNA. (1974), *Production Conditions in Indian Agriculture: A Study Based on Farm Management Surveys*, Cambridge University Press, Cambridge.

—————. (1980), *On Some Issues of Methods in the Analysis of Social Change*, University of Mysore, Mysore.

BHARADWAJ, KRISHNA and P.K. DAS. (1975), 'Tenurial Conditions and Mode of Exploitation: A Study of Some Villages in Orissa', *Economic and Political Weekly*, Vol. 10, Nos. 5–7.

BHARADWAJ, KRISHNA and P.K. DAS. (1975), 'Tenurial Conditions and Mode of Exploitation: A Study of Some Villages in Orissa—Further Notes', *Economic and Political Weekly*, Vol. 10, Nos. 25–26.

BINSWANGER, HANS P. and MARK R. ROSENZWEIG. (1986), 'Behavioural and Material Determinants of Production Relations in Agriculture', *Journal of Development Studies*, Vol. 22, No. 3.

BIRTHAL, PRATAP SINGH and R.P. SINGH. (1991), 'Land-Lease Market, Resource Adjustment and Agricultural Development', *Indian Journal of Agricultural Economics*, Vol. 46, No. 3, July–September.

BLISS, C.J. and N.H. STERN. (1982), *Palanpur: The Economy of an Indian Village*, Oxford University Press, Delhi.

BLYN, GEORGE. (1966), *Agricultural Trends in India, 1891–1947: Output Availability and Productivity in India*, University of Pennsylvania Press, Philadelphia.

BOSE, BUDDHADEB. (1981), 'Agrarian Programme of Left Front Government in West Bengal', *Economic and Political Weekly*, Vol. 16, No. 50, 12 December.

BOSE, SUGATA. (1986), *Agrarian Bengal: Economy, Social Structure and Politics*, Cambridge University Press, Cambridge.

BRAVERMAN, AVISHAY and JOSEPH E. STIGLITZ. (1982), 'Sharecropping and the Interlinking of Agrarian Markets', *American Economic Review*, Vol. 72, No. 4.

————. (1986), 'Cost-Sharing Arrangements and Sharecropping: Moral Hazard, Incentive Flexibility and Risk', *American Journal of Agricultural Economics*, Vol. 68, No. 3.

BRAVERMAN, AVISHAY and J. LUIS GUASCH. (1984), 'Capital Requirements, Screening and Interlinked Sharecropping and Credit Contracts', *Journal of Development Economics*, Vol. 14, April.

BUCHANAN-HAMILTON, FRANCIS. (1883), *A Geographical, Statistical and Historical Description of Dinajpur*, Calcutta.

BYRES, T.J. (1983), 'Historical Perspectives on Sharecropping', *Journal of Peasant Studies*, Vol. 10, Nos. 2–3.

CENSUS OF INDIA. (1951), *Report for West Bengal*, Vol. VI.

————. (1961), *District Census Handbook, Midnapore*, Vol. 1.

————. (1981), *District Census Handbook, Midnapore*.

CHAKRAVARTY, APARAJITA and ASHOK RUDRA. (1973), 'Economic Effects of Tenancy: Some Negative Results', *Economic and Political Weekly*, Vol. 8, No. 28, 14 July.

CHANDRA, NIRMAL K. (1974), 'Farm Efficiency under Semi-Feudalism: A Critique of Marginalist Theories and some Marxist Formulations', *Economic and Political Weekly*, Vol. 9, Nos. 32–34.

CHATTERJEE, PARTHA. (1982), 'Agrarian Structure in Pre-Partition Bengal', in Asok Sen et al. (eds.), *Perspectives in Social Sciences 2: Three Studies on the Agrarian Structure in Bengal*, Oxford University Press, Delhi.

————. (1984), *Bengal, 1920–1947: The Land Question*, K.P. Bagchi & Co., Calcutta.

CHATTOPADHYAY, MANABENDU. (1979), 'Relative Efficiency of Owner and Tenant Cultivation: A Case Study', *Economic and Political Weekly*, Vol. 14, No. 39, 29 September.

CHATTOPADHYAY, MANABENDU and SUMIT KUMAR GHOSH. (1983), 'Tenurial Contracts in a Peasant Movement Belt: Field Survey Data on Naxalbari, Kharibari and Phansidewa Regions', *Economic and Political Weekly*, Vol. 18, No. 26, 25 June.

CHAUDHURI, BINAY BHUSAN. (1969), 'Rural Credit Relation in Bengal, 1859–1885', *Indian Economic and Social History Review*, Vol. 6, No. 3.

CHAUDHURI, BINAY BHUSAN. (1975a), 'Land Market in Eastern India, 1793–1940, Part I: The Movement of Land Prices', *Indian Economic and Social History Review*, Vol. 12, No. 1.

————. (1975b), 'Land Market in Eastern India, 1793–1940, Part II: The Changing Composition of the Landed Society', *Indian Economic and Social History Review*, Vol. 12, No. 2.

————. (1975c), 'The Process of Depeasantisation in Bengal and Bihar, 1885–1947', *Indian Historical Review*, Vol. 2, No. 1.

CHAUDHURI, B. (1982), 'Agrarian Relations: Eastern India', in Dharma Kumar and Tapan Roychaudhuri (eds.), *The Cambridge Economic History of India*, Vol. 2, Orient Longman, Bombay.

CHEUNG, STEVEN N.S. (1969), *The Theory of Share Tenancy*, University of Chicago Press, Chicago.

CHOWDHURY, BENOY K. (1967), 'Agrarian Economy and Agrarian Relations in Bengal, 1859–1885', in Narendra Krishna Sinha (ed.), *Administrative, Economic and Social History of Bengal (1757–1905)*, University of Calcutta, Calcutta.

COOPER, ADRIENNE. (1983), 'Sharecropping and Landlords in Bengal, 1930–50: The Dependency Web and its Implications', *Journal of Peasant Studies*, Vol. 10, Nos. 2–3.

————. (1988), *Sharecropping and Sharecroppers' Struggles in Bengal, 1930–1950*, K.P. Bagchi & Co:, Calcutta.

CURRIE, J.M. (1981), *The Economic Theory of Agricultural Land Tenure*, Cambridge University Press, Cambridge.

DANTWALA, M.L. and C.H. SHAH. (1971), 'Pre-Reform and Post-Reform Agrarian Structure', *Indian Journal of Agricultural Economics*, Vol. 26, No. 3, July–September.

DASGUPTA, BIPLAB. (1973), 'Naxalite Armed Struggles and the Annihilation Campaign in Rural Areas', *Economic and Political Weekly*, Vol. 8, Nos. 4–6, February.

————. (1984a), 'Mode of Production and the Extent of Differentiation in Pre-British Bengal', *Social Scientist*, Vol. 12, No. 8.

————. (1984b), 'Sharecropping in West Bengal during the Colonial Period', *Economic and Political Weekly*, Vol. 19, No. 13, 31 March.

————. (1984c), 'Sharecropping in West Bengal: From Independence to Operation Barga', *Economic and Political Weekly*, Vol. 19, No. 26, 30 June.

————. (1984d), 'Agricultural Labour under Colonial, Semi-Capitalist and Capitalist Conditions: A Case Study of West Bengal', *Economic and Political Weekly*, Vol. 19, 29 September.

————. (1987), *Monitoring and Evaluation of the Agrarian Reform Programme of West Bengal* (mimeo), Calcutta, December.

DATTA, PRABHAT. (1992), *The Second Generation Panchayats in India: With Special Reference to West Bengal*, Calcutta Book House, Calcutta.

DUTT, R.P. (1979), *India Today*, Manisha, Calcutta.

DWIVEDI, HARENDRANATH and ASHOK RUDRA. (1973), 'Economic Effects of Tenancy: Some Further Negative Results', *Economic and Political Weekly*, Vol. 8, No. 29, 21 July.

GHATE, PRABHU et al. (1992), *Informal Finance: Some Findings From Asia*, Asian Development Bank, Manila.

GHOSE, A.K. and A. SAITH. (1976), 'Indebtedness, Tenancy and Adoption of New Technology in Semi-Feudal Agriculture', *World Development*, Vol. 4, April.

GHOSH, A. and K. DUTT. (1977), *Development of Capitalist Relations in Agriculture*, People's Publishing House, New Delhi.

GHOSH, M.G. (1981), 'Impact of New Technology on Land Structure Through Changes in Lease Market: A Study in a Bengal District', *Indian Journal of Agricultural Economics*, Vol. 36, No. 4, October–December.

GHOSH, RATAN. (1981), 'Agrarian Programme of Left Front Government', *Economic and Political Weekly*, Vol. 16, Nos. 25–26, 20–27 June.

GHOSH, TUSHAR KANTI. (1986), *Operation Barga and Land Reforms*, B.R. Publishing Corporation, Delhi.

GOVERNMENT OF BENGAL. (1940), *Report of the Land Revenue Commission*, Vols. I–II.

————. (1941), *Report of the Land Revenue Commission*, Vol. VI.

GOVERNMENT OF INDIA. (1966), *Seminar on Land Reform*. 25–26 February, Socio-Economic Research Division, Planning Commission.

————. (1975), *Report of the National Commission on Agriculture*, Vol. 15.

————. *Satistical Abstract*, various years.

GOVERNMENT OF WEST BENGAL. (1980), *Land Reforms in West Bengal*, Statistical Report IV, Statistical Cell, Board of Revenue.

————. (1980), *Left Front Government and Some of Its Activities in Rural Areas*, June.

————. (1980), *From Santal Insurrection to Operation Barga* (in Bengali), June.

————. (1982), *Guidelines for Bank Financing to Sharecroppers and Patta Holders*.

————. *Economic Review*, various years.

————. *Satistical Abstract*, various years.

GRIFFIN, KEITH. (1974), *The Political Economy of Agrarian Change: An Essay on the Green Revolution*, Macmillan, London.

HABIB, IRFAN. (1982), 'Agrarian Economy' in Tapan Roychaudhuri and Dharma Kumar (eds.), *The Cambridge Economic History of India*, Vol. 1, Orient Longman, Bombay.

HALLAGAN, WILLIAM. (1978), 'Self-selection by Contractual Choice and the Theory of Sharecropping', *Bell Journal of Economics*, Vol. 9, Autumn.

HAQUE, T. (1987), 'Temporal and Regional Variations in the Agrarian Structure in India', *Indian Journal of Agricultural Economics*, Vol. 42, No. 3, July–September.

HAQUE, T. and G. PARTHASARATHY. (1992), 'Land Reform and Rural Development: Highlights of a National Seminar', *Economic and Political Weekly*, Vol. 27, No. 8, 22 February.

HEADY, EARL O. (1947), 'Economics of Farm Leasing Systems', *Journal of Farm Economics*, August.

HOSSAIN, MAHABUB. (1977), 'Farm Size, Tenancy and Land Productivity: An Analysis of Farm Level Data in Bangladesh Agriculture', *Bangladesh Development Studies*, Vol. 5, No. 3.

HSIAO, J.C. (1975), 'The Theory of Share Tenancy Revisited', *Journal of Political Economy*, Vol. 83, No. 5.

HUANG, YUKON. (1975), 'Tenancy Patterns, Productivity, and Rentals in Malaysia', *Economic Development and Cultural Change*, Vol. 23, No. 4.

HUNTER, W.W. (1876), *A Statistical Account of Bengal*, Truber and Co., London.

JABBAR, M.A. (1977), 'Relative Productive Efficiency of Different Tenure Classes in Selected Areas of Bangladesh', *Bangladesh Development Studies*, Vol. 13, No. 4.

JAYNES, GERALD D. (1982), 'Production and Distribution in Agrarian Economies', *Oxford Economic Papers*, Vol. 34, No. 2.

JODHA, N.S. (1981), 'Agricultural Tenancy: Fresh Evidence from Dryland Areas in India', *Economic and Political Weekly*, Vol. 16, No. 52, December.

JOHNSON, D. GALE. (1950), 'Resource Allocation Under Share Contracts', *Journal of Political Economy*, Vol. 58, No. 2, April.

JUNANKAR, P.N. (1989), 'The Response of Peasant Farmers to Price Incentives: The Use and Misuse of Profit Functions', *Journal of Development Studies*, Vol. 25, No. 2.

KHASNABIS, RATAN. (1981), 'Operation Barga: Limits to Social Democratic Reformism', *Economic and Political Weekly*, Vol. 16, Nos. 25–26, 20–27 June.

—————. (1982), 'Operation Barga: A Further Note', *Economic and Political Weekly*, Vol. 17, No. 26, 4 September.

KHASNABIS, RATAN and JYOTIPRAKASH CHAKRAVORTY. (1982), 'Tenancy, Credit and Agrarian Backwardness: Results of a Field Survey', *Economic and Political Weekly*, Vol. 17, No. 13, 27 March.

LIETEN, G.K. (1990), 'Depeasantisation Discontinued: Land Reforms in West Bengal', *Economic and Political Weekly*, Vol. 25, No. 40, 6 October.

LUCAS, ROBERT E.B. (1979), 'Sharing, Monitoring and Incentives: Marshallian Misallocation Reassessed', *Journal of Political Economy*, Vol. 87, No. 3.

MAITY, SUBHRENDU. (1978), 'Agrarian Unrest: A Case Study on the Naxalite Movement in Midnapore, West Bengal', *Man and Life*, Vol. 4, Nos. 1–4.

MAJID, NOMAAN. (1988), 'The Method of Usury and Accumulation of Backward Agriculture: A Methodological Discussion of Bhaduri's Thesis', *Journal of Peasant Studies*, Vol. 15, No. 2.

MANLY, BRYAN F.J. (1986), *Multivariate Statistical Methods*, Chapman and Hall, London.

MARSHALL, AFLRED. (1890), *Principles of Economics*, Macmillan, London, 1920 edition.

MITRA, PRADEEP K. (1983), 'A Theory of Interlinked Rural Transactions', *Journal of Public Economics*, Vol. 20, No. 2.

MUKHERJEE, RAMAKRISHNA. (1957), *Dynamics of Rural Society*, Akademie-Verlag, Berlin.

MURTY, C.S. (1987), 'Influence of Socio-Economic Status on Contractual Terms of Tenancy: A Study in Two Delta Villages of Andhra Pradesh', *Economic and Political Weekly*, Vol. 22, No. 39, September.

NABI, IZAZ. (1985), 'Rural Factor Market Imperfections and the Incidence of Tenancy in Agriculture', *Oxford Economic Papers*, Vol. 37, No. 2.

—————. (1986), 'Contracts, Resource Use and Productivity in Sharecropping', *Journal of Development Studies*, Vol. 22, No. 2.

NADKARNI, M.V. (1976), 'Tenants From the Dominant Class: A Developing Contradiction in Land Reforms', *Economic and Political Weekly*, Vol. 11, No. 52, December.

NEWBERY, D.M.G. (1975), 'Tenurial Obstacles to Innovation', *Journal of Development Studies*, Vol. 11, No. 4.

—————. (1977), 'Risk Sharing, Sharecropping and Uncertain Labour Markets', *Review of Economic Studies*, Vol. 44, No. 138.

OTSUKA, KEIJIRO *et al.* (1992), 'Land and Labour Contracts in Agrarian Economies: Theories and Facts', *Journal of Economic Literature*, Vol. 30, No. 4, December.

PANT, CHANDRAKANT. (1983), 'Tenancy and Family Resources: A Model and Some Empirical Analysis', *Journal of Development Economics*, Vol. 12, Nos. 1–2.

PATEL, SURENDRA J. (1952), *Agricultural Labourers in Modern India and Pakistan*, Current Book House, Bombay.

PATNAIK, UTSA. (1987), *Peasant Class Differentiation: A Study in Method with Reference to Haryana*, Oxford University Press, Delhi.

PEARCE, R. (1983), 'Sharecropping: Towards a Marxist View', *Journal of Peasant Studies*, Vol. 10, Nos. 2–3.

PRASAD, PRADHAN H. (1973), 'Production Relations: Achilles' Heel of Indian Planning', *Economic and Political Weekly*, Vol. 8, No. 19, 12 May.

—————. (1974), 'Reactionary Role of Usurer's Capital in Rural India', *Economic and Political Weekly*, Vol. 9, Nos. 32–34, Special Number.

RAJ, K.N. (1979), 'Keynesian Economics and Agrarian Economies', in C.H.H. Rao and P.C. Joshi (eds.), *Reflections on Economic Development and Social Change: Essays in Honour of V.K.R.V. Rao*, Allied Publishers, Delhi.

RAO, C.H. HANUMANTHA. (1971), 'Uncertainty, Entrepreneurship, and Sharecropping in India', *Journal of Political Economy*, Vol. 79, No. 3.

RAO, V.M. (1972), 'Land Transfer in Rural Communities: Some Findings in a Ryotwari Region', *Economic and Political Weekly*, Vol. 12, No. 40, September.

—————. (1974), 'Village Lease Markets for Agricultural Land: Some Approaches for Analysis', *Economic and Political Weekly*, Vol. 9, No. 26, June.

RAY, DEBIDAS. (1978), 'The Small Lessor and the Big Lessee: Evidence from West Bengal', *Economic and Political Weekly*, Vol. 13, Nos. 51–52, 23–30 December.

REID, JR. JOSEPH D. (1973), 'Sharecropping As an Understandable Market Response: The Post-Bellum South', *Journal of Economic History*, Vol. 33, No. 1.
——————. (1976), 'Sharecropping and Agricultural Uncertainty', *Economic Development and Cultural Change*, Vol. 24, No. 3.
——————. (1977), 'The Theory of Share Tenancy Revisited Again', *Journal of Political Economy*, Vol. 85, No. 2.
REDDY, M.V. NARAYANA. (1992), 'Interlinkages of Credit with Factor and Product Markets: A Study in Andhra Pradesh', *Indian Journal of Agricultural Economics*, Vol. 47, No. 4, October–December.
RESERVE BANK OF INDIA. (1984), *Agricultural Productivty in Eastern India*, Vols. I-II.
RUDRA, ASHOK. (1975*a*), 'Loans as Part of Agrarian Relations: Some Results of a Preliminary Survey in West Bengal', *Economic and Political Weekly*, Vol. 10, 12 July.
——————. (1975*b*), 'Sharecropping Arrangements in West Bengal', *Economic and Political Weekly*, Vol. 10, 27 September.
——————. (1981), 'One Step Forward and Two Steps Backward', *Economic and Political Weekly*, Vol. 16, Nos. 25–26, 20–27 June.
——————. (1982), *Indian Agricultural Economics: Myths and Realities*, Allied Publishers, Delhi.
——————. (1988), 'Emerging Class Structure in Rural India' in T.N. Srinivasan and Pranab K. Bardhan (eds.), *Rural Poverty in South Asia*, Oxford University Press, Delhi.
——————. (1992), *Political Economy of Indian Agriculture*, K.P. Bagchi & Co., Calcutta.
SANYAL, S.K. (1988), 'Trends in Landholding and Poverty in Rural India', in T.N. Srinivasan and Pranab K. Bardhan (eds.), *Rural Poverty in South Asia*, Oxford University Press, Delhi.
SARAP, KAILAS. (1991), *Interlined Agrarian Markets in Rural India*, Sage Publications, New Delhi.
SAU, RANJIT. (1975), 'Farm Efficiency Under Semi-Feudalism: A Critique of Marginalist Theories and Some Marxist Formulations—A Comment', *Economic and Political Weekly*, Vol. 10, No. 13.
SCHIEKELE, RAINER. (1941), 'Effects of Tenure Systems on Agricultural Efficiency', *Journal of Farm Economics*, February.
SCHILLER, OTTO. (1957), *Cooperative Farming and Individual Farming on Cooperative Lines*, AICU, New Delhi.
SEN, ASOK. (1982), 'Agrarian Structure and Tenancy Laws in Bengal, 1850–1900' in Asok Sen et al. (eds.), *Perspectives in Social Sciences 2: Three Studies on the Agrarian Structure in Bengal*, Oxford University Press, Delhi.
SEN, BHOWANI.(1962), *Evolution of Agrarian Relations in India*, People's Publishing House, New Dehi.
SEN, SUNIL. (1972), *Agrarian Struggle in Bengal, 1946–47*, People's Publishing House, New Delhi.
——————. (1979), *Agrarian Relations in India, 1793–1947*, People's Publishing House, New Delhi.
SENGUPTA, SUNIL. (1981), 'West Bengal Land Reforms and the Agrarian Scene', *Economic and Political Weekly*, Vol. 16, Nos. 25–26, 20–27 June.

SHABAN, RADWAN ALI. (1987), 'Testing Between Competing Models of Share-cropping', *Journal of Political Economy*, Vol. 95, No. 5.

SINGH, IQBAL. (1989), 'Reverse Tenancy in Punjab Agriculture: Impact of Techno-logical Change', *Economic and Political Weekly*, Vol. 24, No. 25, 24 June.

SINHA, NARENDRA KRISHNA. (1968), *The Economic History of Bengal*, Vol. 2, Firma K.L. Mukhopadhyay, Calcutta.

SMITH, ADAM. (1776), *An Inquiry Into the Nature and Causes of the Wealth of Nations*, Encyclopaedia Britanica Inc., Chicago, 1952 edition.

STIGLITZ, JOSEPH E. (1974), 'Incentives and Risk Sharing in Sharecropping', *Review of Economic Studies*, Vol. 41, April.

————. (1986), 'New Development Economics', *World Development*, Vol. 14, No. 2.

SUTINEN, J.C. (1975), 'The Rational Choice of Share Leasing and Implications for Efficiency', *American Journal of Agricultural Economics*, Vol. 57, No. 4, November.

SWAMY, DILIP S. (1988), 'Agricultural Tenancy in the 1970s', *Indian Journal of Agricultural Economics*, Vol. 43, No. 4, October–December.

TASLIM, M.A. (1988), 'Tenancy and Interlocking Markets: Issues and Some Evi-dence', *World Development*, Vol. 16, No. 6.

THORNER, DANIEL and ALICE THORNER. (1962), *Land and Labour in India*, Asia Publishing House, Bombay.

VYAS, V.S. (1970), 'Tenancy in a Dynamic Setting', *Economic and Political Weekly*, Vol. 5, No. 26, 27 June.

ZAMAN, M. RAQUIBUZ. (1973), 'Sharecropping and Economic Efficiency in Bangla-desh', *Bangladesh Economic Review*, Vol. 1, No. 2.